proclamation

**Interpreting
the Lessons
of the
Church Year**

Philip H. Pfatteicher

HOLY WEEK

From The Desk Of
Judy Doll

D1568330

PROCLAMATION 6 | SERIES B

FORTRESS PRESS | MINNEAPOLIS

PROCLAMATION 6
Interpreting the Lessons of the Church Year
Series B, Holy Week

Cover design: Ellen Maly
Text design: David Lott

The Library of Congress has cataloged the first four volumes of Series A as follows:

Proclamation 6, Series A: interpreting the lessons of the church
    year.
            p.   cm.
        Contents: [1] Advent/Christmas / J. Christiaan Beker — [2]
    Epiphany / Susan K. Hedahl — [3] Lent / Peter J. Gomes — [4] Holy
    Week / Robin Scroggs.
        ISBN 0-8006-4207-4 (v. 1 : alk. paper) — ISBN 0-8006-4208-2 (v.
    2 : alk. paper) — ISBN 0-8006-4209-0 (v. 3 : alk. paper) — ISBN 0-8006-4210-4
    (v. 4 : alk. paper).
        1. Bible—Homiletical use. 2. Bible—liturgical lessons,
    English.
    BS534.5P74   1995
    251—dc20   95-4622
                                                                           CIP
            Series B:
            Advent/Christmas / Arthur J. Dewey—ISBN 0-8006-4215-5
            Epiphany / Mark Allan Powell—ISBN 0-8006-4216-3
            Lent / James H. Harris, Miles Jerome Jones, and Jerome C. Ross—
                    ISBN 0-8006-4217-1
            Holy Week / Philip H. Pfatteicher—ISBN 0-8006-4218-X
            Easter / Beverly R. Gaventa—ISBN 0-8006-4219-8
            Pentecost 1 / Ched Myers—ISBN 0-8006-4220-1
            Pentecost 2 / Richard L. Eslinger—ISBN 0-8006-4221-X
            Pentecost 3 / Laura Lagerquist-Gottwald and Norman K. Gottwald—
                    ISBN 0-8006-4222-8

The paper used in this publication meets the minimum requirements of American National
Standard for Information Sciences—Permanence of Paper for Printed Library Materials,
ANSI Z329.48-1948.

Manufactured in the U. S. A.   AF 1-4218

00   99   98   97   96   1   2   3   4   5   6   7   8   9   10

Contents

Introduction

The Great and Holy Week takes its name from the great and holy deeds it commemorates. This central week of the Christian year is the church's way of proclaiming and re-experiencing the events that changed the world.

Honest people, however, will find that claim about the events of Holy Week troubling, for the world as we see and experience it seems little different from the way it was before the crucifixion. The English poet and novelist Thomas Hardy, in his poem "Christmas: 1924," lamented,

> After two thousand years of mass
> We've got as far as poison gas.

Since then the world has experienced the Holocaust and atomic bombs on Hiroshima and Nagasaki. If anything, the world has gotten worse since the first Christmas. The task of proclamation during Holy Week is to confront that apparent lack of change and to show how the events celebrated during this week are in fact central to human history.

The approach lies not just in the assertion of personal security and salvation but in the recognition of what religion at its best does. The purpose of religion is to push back the boundaries of the world, to expand the horizon of reality. From a limited human perspective, the world has not changed after the death and resurrection of Christ. But this Great and Holy Week enlarges our understanding of what went on then and what continues to go on in the present time. The combat between death and life occurs in places and ways one might not expect. How have the crucifixion and its surrounding events changed your life and the lives of the people to whom you preach? That is the basic question the great and holy week raises. More than any other time in the Christian year, this week demands spiritual preparation of the preacher before any convincing sermon can be delivered.

The preacher, rather than being overwhelmed by the task, should take heart. This week above all the other weeks of the year is celebrated with remarkably rich liturgical actions that enhance and reinforce the biblical texts. The preacher needs to take into careful consideration the liturgical setting of the readings and sermons, for the liturgies give considerable guidance and help in the responsible interpretation and proclamation of the readings. These liturgies and readings mutually interpret each other.

The preacher this week has abundant and specific help. The liturgies for Holy Week abound in texts such as prayers, antiphons, and anthems, as well as actions that guide the interpreter in understanding how the biblical readings have been understood through the ages and applied to the experience of Christian people. This week a conservative approach commends itself. It is not a time for extended speculation about the authenticity of certain problematic biblical texts; there is time enough for that at other times in the year and in settings other than the pulpit. This week is the time to recall the Christian people to the heart and center of the faith: the unitive event of the death and resurrection of Jesus Christ, the Son of God.

The Sunday of the Passion
Palm Sunday

Lectionary	First Lesson	Psalm	Second Lesson	Gospel
Revised Common	Isa. 50:4-9a	Ps. 31:9-16	Phil. 2:5-11	Mark 14:1—15:47 or 15:1-39 (40-47)
Episcopal (BCP)	Isa. 45:21-25 or Isa. 52:13—53:12	Ps. 22:1-21 or 22:1-11	Phil. 2:5-11	Mark (14:32-72) or 15:1-39 (40-47)
Roman Catholic	Isa. 50:4-7	Ps. 22:8-9, 17-20, 23-24	Phil. 2:6-11	Mark 14:1—15:47 or Mark 15:1-39
Lutheran (LBW)	Zech. 9:9-10	Ps. 31:1-5, 9-16	Phil. 2:5-11	Mark 14:1—15:47 or Mark 15:1-39

Holy Week begins with the Sunday of the Passion. *Now* Passiontide begins, the intense and exclusive concentration on the suffering and death of our Lord Jesus Christ. It has in the past been the custom of many, particularly Lutherans, to make all of Lent a remembrance of the passion; nails and whips and the crown of thorns are symbols frequently but erroneously associated with Lent. The ancient and still appropriate focus of Lent is baptism and its implications for daily living. Holy Week is the appropriate and useful time for attention to the cross. This attention is intense, limited to one week, and it is exclusive, for no other celebrations are appropriate during this time. No holy days that may fall during this week are celebrated, no weddings. All that can be postponed is moved out of these seven days (in fact moved out of the next seven also, Easter Week) to make room only for the meditation and reflection upon the suffering and death of the Son of God.

The palm ceremonies, which are a popular and conspicuous feature of this Sunday, have been so prominent as to give the familiar name to the day, "Palm Sunday." The ceremonies involve distributing palm (and other) branches to the congregation, reading the Gospel account (Mark 11:1-11 this year; or, an option given in the Roman Catholic and Revised Common lectionaries, John 12:12-16) of Jesus' triumphal entry into Jerusalem at the beginning of the week, and dramatizing that entry by processing with palms and singing the ninth-century hymn, "All glory, laud, and honor/To thee, Redeemer, King!" The procession, in which the congregation often participates, whether going to the church building or around it or within it, is an act of praise to Christ the king, a sovereign who reigns and triumphs paradoxically on the tree of the cross. The procession is also an expression of willingness to take up the cross and follow the Lord of glory along the way of sorrows, through death to the life that lies beyond. The introductory procession with palms is an announcement of the theme of victory over the forces of sin and death, which is the grand and overarching theme of this great week.

If these ceremonies are understood and done well, they set the tone and the approach for all that is to be done this week. It is far more than a recalling of events that happened centuries ago on the other side of a vastly different world. The words of the prophet Zechariah (the first lesson in the Lutheran lectionary) ring through this celebration and announce its central theme: "Your king comes to you; triumphant and victorious is he" (Zech. 9:9). The words of the prophet leap from the original address to ancient Israel and speak directly to us. The king, our king, comes to us. This week is the culmination of God's coming to humanity in power and might, concealed in humility and apparent weakness. This concealed power is more than a trick, a deception to catch the devil, as some ancient commentators suggested. It is in fact humility that *reveals* the might of God. The triumphant and victorious king rides not on a horse, not in a chariot, but on a beast of burden, a donkey. Such is God's way of working the transformation of the world.

We cannot understand it yet, if this story is all we know. We need the events of the entire week, taken together, to be able to see the meaning of what Jesus was acting out in this entrance. The great king (Zech. 9:9; John 12:13,15) was coming into "the city of the great King" (Ps. 48:2), riding on "a colt that has never been ridden" (cf. Luke 23:53; John 19:41). As John's account of the triumphal entry explains, "His disciples did not understand these things at first; but when Jesus was glorified, then they remembered that these things had been written of him and had been done to him" (John 12:16).

The procession with palms, therefore, is but the introduction to the purpose of the day: the proclamation of the passion of Christ, this year according to Mark. On this first day of the week, the day of resurrection, we read about how Jesus died. That story is not reserved until Good Friday. In the richness of Christian worship and celebration we are not just walking in Jesus' steps from entrance (Sunday) to controversy (Monday and Tuesday) to betrayal (Wednesday and Thursday) to death (Friday) to resurrection (Sunday). We do that, but in a complex way, for today, this Sunday of the Passion, we ponder what it means that the lowly king came to die. And no account of the death of Jesus makes it more terrifying than this year's Gospel, the Gospel of Mark. It was by dying that this king revealed and worked his victorious and triumphant power.

FIRST LESSON: ISAIAH 50:4-9a; 45:21-25

But first we must attend to the first two readings that prepare for the long Gospel. In the church's story, nothing stands alone. Everything is part of a large and richly textured story. The first lesson in the Roman Catholic and the Revised Common lectionaries is from the prophet Isaiah, the Third Servant Song (**Isa. 50:4-9a**). When Christians read the Servant Songs it is impossible for them not to hear in the words of this servant of God the voice of Jesus. Here, more than anywhere else perhaps, Christians find that Christ has clarified and fulfilled the mysterious ancient words which in their original setting could refer to a coming Messiah or the whole people of Israel or a contemporary but unrecognized figure or a poetic creation to focus the meaning of servanthood. (All of these have been advanced from time to time to identify the Servant.) But read on this Sunday, in a Christian church, it is Christ who is heard to say, "I was not rebellious . . . I gave my back to those who struck me . . . I did not hide my face from insult and spitting." A representative of the United States, visiting some "underdeveloped" country, is spit on, and America is enraged at such contempt, for the official represents us. But in Isaiah's song, the reaction of the servant is quite different and unexpected: "I have not been disgraced." The shame rather is theirs who show this holy servant such contempt and who give such brutal treatment. For all the enemies can do, the servant is unmoved, showing the ultimate weakness of such violent power. Their rage is not "manly" but childish; it may terrify, but it does not finally accomplish anything. Moreover, the confident assertion of the servant is that the one "who vindicates me is near." God has not abandoned the servant, and with that knowledge the servant can taunt those who do the violence, "Let them confront me. It is the Lord GOD who helps me." And in that contest God's victory is sure. The confidence of the servant, notice carefully, is not the taunt of the fighter, "Come at me if you dare; I can demolish you all." The servant's confidence is not in his own might but in the Lord God. He is aware of his status as a servant of one whose power alone makes all the difference, a power concealed in apparent weakness.

The reading appointed by the *Book of Common Prayer*, **Isa. 45:21-25**, makes a similar point: "Only in the LORD . . . are righteousness and strength." The events commemorated during this holy week demonstrate that in God alone is strength and victory: "There is no other god besides me; a righteous God and a Savior; there is no one besides me." It is an exclusive and overwhelming claim of a living monotheism: there is no other God. All that the world offers and honors—beauty and youth and wealth and aggressiveness—must ultimately fail and disappoint and betray. "There is no one besides me," declares the creator, the Holy One, and in the end "to me every knee shall bow, every tongue shall swear [allegiance]" (see the second lesson for this day). Again, it is not the demand of a megalomaniac tyrant, for the requirement of obedience is not for God's good but for ours. "In the LORD all the offspring of Israel shall triumph and glory." The victory of Christ, this week proclaims, was on our behalf, and in that victory *we* are triumphant.

SECOND LESSON: PHILIPPIANS 2:5-11

The second lesson (epistle) for this Sunday since ancient times has been the wonderful Song of the Humility of Christ, Phil. 2:5-11. It is the second lesson in each of the three years of the lectionary cycle. Again we are to learn that the mind of Christ is to be ours as well. We are this week not like spectators watching a movie or a play or a sports event. We are participants in the events we commemorate, and if we do not find ourselves in these events we have not yet begun to understand Holy Week. "Let the same mind be in you that was in Christ Jesus." We are not simply to be like Christ, to imitate Christ; we are to share his very nature and being. His mind, intention, purpose are to be ours. We are not just to become like him; we are in fact to become so like Christ that our life and his become indistinguishable. He poured himself out for us—literally by draining his lifeblood on the cross—and we are to do likewise, draining ourselves of every drop of self-interest and self-concern and pride and to become slaves, wholly and gladly obedient to Another.

Then, when we have accomplished this, comes the exaltation. The way up, we learn, is the way down, the way of exaltation is the way of humiliation. Death must come before glory, the cross before the crown. The grand vision of this soaring reading is that one day everyone and everything will bow in homage before Christ the King and acknowledge that the crucified and risen and ascended and reigning Christ bears nothing less than the title of Israel's God: Jesus Christ is LORD.

GOSPEL: MARK 14:1—15:47 (15:1-39)

Thus we are prepared by the first lesson and the second lesson to hear the Gospel, the passion of our Lord Jesus Christ according to Mark. The characteristic features of Mark are, as one might expect, to be found in the passion account: simplicity, few Old Testament quotations, swift-moving action, attention to detail. Mark's Gospel, which has been a "gospel of power" because of its emphasis on Jesus' miracles, draws near its close with Jesus dying, apparently abandoned. The "messianic secret" is at last revealed in a paradoxical way now that the story is nearly all told, and the revelation is made by a Roman centurion.

The daunting question for the preacher is how to deal with such a large body of Scripture as the two long chapters of the passion account. The preacher cannot deal with all of it in a detailed way, of course.

One approach could be to examine one or more of the distinctive Markan passages in the account, but other than a few specific details there are no passages that are Mark's own. One is the brief appearance of the nameless young man who fled naked from the scene of Jesus' arrest (Mark 14:51-52). He may be the evangelist himself, the signature of the evange- list. The passage may echo Gen. 39:12 (Joseph was thrown into the dun- geon and was later resurrected) or Amos 2:16. The man may suggest can- didates for baptism who enter the font naked to die with Christ and are then raised to life with him.

Mark alone identifies Simon of Cyrene as the father of Alexander and Rufus. Perhaps this Rufus is the one mentioned by Paul as "chosen in the Lord," who was a member of the church in Rome (Rom. 16:13). The role of Peter in this passion account could be related to the report of the sec- ond-century bishop Papias who called Mark "the interpreter of Peter."

There is a distinctive emphasis, characteristic of Mark's story, that is perhaps more promising for the preacher. As Mark recounts the passion, Jesus is increasingly isolated and alone. First Judas goes to the chief priests and, with their promise of money, "began to look for an opportunity to betray him" (14:11). On the Mount of Olives Jesus says to the disciples, "You will all become deserters," as was foretold by Zechariah (13:7). Peter and all the disciples refused to admit that they could betray Jesus. Peter, James, and John fell asleep three times, as Jesus prayed in the garden appropriately named Gethsemane ("oil press"). When Jesus was arrested, "all of them deserted him and fled." Peter followed to the high priest's courtyard, but there, while Jesus was being beaten, denied three times that he knew Jesus. Pilate "realized that it was out of jealousy that the chief priests had handed him over," but he quickly caved in to their demand for crucifixion, and Mark makes the devastating comment, "wishing to satisfy the crowd." Jesus had been beaten before; now he is ridiculed. A king crowned with thorns, wearing a cloak of royal purple, struck, spit on, and mockingly worshiped, Jesus goes to his death not wearing the garments of mockery but his own clothes. Ordinary clothing is fit for this humble king. Simon of Cyrene was the only one who did anything for Jesus, but he was "compelled" to do so. He did not share willingly in carrying the cross. Jesus is crucified between two bandits, but unlike John's account they both join the chief priests in taunting Jesus. Finally, in the strange darkness at noonday, at three in the afternoon, Jesus cries out, "My God, why have you forsaken me?" It is the only word from the cross in this Gospel. And with that most terrifying cry in all Scripture, he dies. Jesus is increasingly isolated and rejected. He dies isolated from his followers, the priests of his religion, the people, the two executed with him. Isolated from the human race, at last he is abandoned even by God, who, he cries, has forsaken him. With a final, desolate scream ("loud cry" in the restrained language of the Gospel), Jesus dies. It is an utterly terrifying picture.

It looks like defeat, a complete collapse, a surrender to darkness, despair, and utter solitude and desolation. We may know something of such suffering in our own lives—lying on a bed of pain, sitting stunned by a devastating loss, walking too pained to cry. Suffering for us can be a defeat and complete surrender, dying physically and spiritually.

Yet, for Jesus (and for us) that is not all. Mark's passion account, for all of its desolation and terror, victory is never far away. The final, frightening cry does not echo and fade across the hills outside Jerusalem. It tears the curtain of the temple in two, from top to bottom, and it moved the centurion in charge of the execution, who saw not only that he died but how he died, to confess, "Truly this man was God's Son." A centurion confirms the Gospel which began, one should remember, "The beginning of the good news of Jesus Christ, the Son of God" (Mark 1:1), an idea repeated at Jesus' baptism and at his transfiguration. To a soldier whom we imagine to be hardened to execution and death, this death was compellingly different. No mortal had died in quite this way before. Here, dead on the cross, was no criminal abandoned and rejected by family and friends and everyone. Here was one whose death proclaimed his divinity. He died like God.

God, as Alexander Schmemann explains in *For the Life of the World: Sacraments and Orthodoxy* (Crestwood, N.Y.: St. Vladimir's, 1973), is not the last resort to stop the awful pain, not a replacement for medicine that has exhausted its possibilities. God is life itself. Christ's dying is in fact the victory of life, confirmed and sealed by the resurrection. Everything therefore must come through the last darkness to God and ascend to the fullness of love. When the church, born from this awe-full event, ministers to the sick it does so not merely to comfort them, not only to help them, but to make them martyrs, bound to the passion of Christ, witnesses to Christ in their very suffering and desolation.

It is not a priest who sees that, not one learned in the law and theologically trained, not a Jew at all, but an outsider, a Gentile, the Roman centurion. This fact suggests another characteristic of this passion account (which it shares with Luke): This is a story for all humanity. Everyone is capable of understanding the significance of this death. It has meaning not just for one group but for all. At the beginning of Mark's passion account, Jesus says of the woman who anointed his head with oil, "Wherever the good news is proclaimed in the whole world, what she has done will be told in remembrance of her" (14:9). When the woman in her generosity has anointed Jesus, Judas (the very next event so that we do not miss its significance), acting on his own, goes to the chief priests and in his self-ishness, lured by their offer of money, "began to look for an opportunity to betray him" (v. 11). Two days later, Jesus sat at another table, and this time, instead of a woman's generous act, had to endure a man's betrayal. The woman's action is highly praised in words that echo those we associ-ate with the Lord's Supper, "in remembrance of her." Indeed, in the Gospel accounts the words Paul connected with the supper (1 Cor. 11:23-25), "in remembrance of me," are not used in connection with the supper. Mark applies then instead to the woman who anointed Jesus beforehand for his burial.

The principal themes of Mark's Gospel come to a focus in the passion narrative. In Gethsemane, we who watch Jesus in his last hours learn first of all of his obedience to the Father's will. He was completely human, and, knowing what surely lay ahead even this night, he prayed for deliverance: "remove this cup from me" (14:36). It is the cup of suffering (cf. Mark 10:38; Isa. 51:17; Lam. 4:21). Jesus did not want to die. No healthy person does. But then comes the powerful reversal. "Yet not what I want, but what you want." Later, he accepts his arrest not with resignation but with an affirmation and interpretation, "Let the scriptures be fulfilled" (14:49). The cup remains, but it is filled with profound meaning. It is not only the cup of suffering and death; it is the cup of the Lord's Supper, the blood poured out for many (that is to say, for all), which becomes the cup of life and salva-tion (Ps. 16:5; 116:13).

Jesus' submissive obedience to the will of the Father is in sharp contrast to the response of the disciples. Jesus commanded them, "Keep awake," and they fell asleep. They, shamefully, did that three times. Their spiritual blindness has been emphasized throughout Mark's Gospel (4:13, 40, 41; 6:50-52; 7:18; 8:16-21; 9:5ff.; 10:35-40).

This already indicates the second Markan theme found in this incident: the theme of watchfulness. The disciples' inability to keep awake suggests not only their exhaustion, their blindness to what is happening. It brings to a shameful climax the warnings about the end heard earlier in this Gospel at the conclusion of the "little apocalypse," just before the passion account opens. "Keep awake—for you do not know when the master of the house will come, in the evening, or at midnight, or at cockcrow, or at dawn, or else he may find you asleep when he comes suddenly" (13:35-36).

The great story of this day, the Sunday of the Passion, the celebration of which began with the exuberant but shadowed procession with palms, now concludes with the burial of "the one who comes in the name of the Lord." He was indeed dead. Three women saw him die; two of them "saw where the body was laid," and the three returned to the tomb Easter morning. Moreover, their eyewitness is confirmed not only by "a respected member of the council" (15:43), Joseph of Arimathea, who asked Pilate for the body of Jesus for burial, but also by the skeptical Pilate, who ascertains from the centurion who supervised the execution, that Jesus was in fact dead, "dead for some time" (v. 44). There could be no mistake. The body that alive was anointed "beforehand for burial" as the passion narrative began, now dead is wrapped in its linen shroud for burial. The Son of God lies in the tomb. But the week has only begun. The story has not yet all been told.

Monday in Holy Week

Lectionary	First Lesson	Psalm	Second Lesson	Gospel
Revised Common	Isa. 42:1-9	Ps. 36:5-11	Heb. 9:11-15	John 12:1-11
Episcopal (BCP)	Isa. 42:1-9	Ps. 36:5-10	Heb. 11:39—12:3	John 12:1-11 or Mark 14:3-9
Roman Catholic	Isa. 42:1-7			John 12:1-11
Lutheran (LBW)	Isa. 42:1-9	Ps. 36:5-10	Heb. 9:11-15	John 12:1-11

The chronological commemoration observed liturgically today is described in the Gospel, "Six days before the Passover." Monday is not six days from the Passover that was celebrated by Jesus on Thursday (or Friday in John's chronology). Monday is, however, six days from Easter Sunday, the Christian Passover, and this suggests how the phrase is to be understood in its present setting. All three lessons serve all three years of the lectionary cycle for Monday in Holy Week.

FIRST LESSON: ISAIAH 42:1-9

The first lesson is the First Song of the Servant given in Isaiah, together with God's comment on the words of the servant. Whatever the identity of this servant in the original context in Isaiah—it may well be the whole nation of Israel—read in Christian churches, especially this week, it inevitably points to Christ, who gathers into himself and into his experience all the promise and experience of ancient Israel and brings them to a climactic focus in his life, death, and resurrection.

The gentleness of this servant, who will not break a slender and bruised reed or quench the barely glowing lamp wick, contrasts sharply with the violence done to him and with his desolate death. The contrast is even sharper between his abandonment on the cross and the Lord God, who says, "Here is my servant, whom I uphold, my chosen, in whom my soul delights." God says of him who died abandoned with a forsaken cry, "He will not grow faint or be crushed until he has established justice in the earth." This Servant Song seems at first sight not to fit well with the passion according to Mark, read yesterday. But God's comment on the servant is not only, "See, the former things have come to pass," as the servant gathers into himself the hopes and fears of his people who longed for him. God also announces, "New things I now declare." What is happening in the passion is a revelation of the revolutionary way and love of God. "I have taken you by the hand and kept you," God says. Such keeping and care, it is now clear, does not mean preserving the servant (nation and person) from even the most intense suffering. It is not a life of ease or security that is promised.

Here are words to set beside the terrifying picture of the passion that Mark presents, words that interpret what is going on. The lonely death is not only terrifying. More profoundly, it is the revelation of the care of God that can embrace and even use desolation and death. Such is the character of the justice that this servant is called to establish. What God does is beyond our understanding, beyond our categories of good and bad, but what God chooses to do is profoundly *right*. "I am the LORD, that is my name; my glory I give to no other." The sovereignty of God is absolute.

The one who dies in the darkness of desolation, by that lonely act, brings light to the nations. Eyes that closed in death did so in order to open the eyes of the blind. The servant who entered the dark prison of the grave did so to "bring out the prisoners from the dungeon, and from the prison those who sit in darkness." The depths of human grief, woe, and despair have been not only understood but entered by the servant of God so that no one who must go down into such dungeons goes there alone. We can hear God say to us as to the servant, "I have taken you by the hand and kept you."

SECOND LESSON: HEBREWS 9:11-15; 11:39—12:3

The second lesson provided by the *Lutheran Book of Worship* and the Revised Common Lectionary is **Heb. 9:11-15**. It is an explication of the meaning of the death of Christ proclaimed in the Gospel for the Sunday of the Passion and for Good Friday. The liturgy for Monday in Holy Week, we are to learn, is more than a chronological walking with Christ through the last days of his life. It is, more than anything, a sustained meditation upon the significance of that awesome death. So this lesson connects most of all not with the first lesson or today's Gospel but with the theme of the week: that passion and death of the Savior of the world.

Here is the Lamb of God, the pure sacrifice, in the profundity of his great and saving work. When Jesus died, the curtain of the temple was torn in two. Like the other two Synoptic evangelists, Mark reports the event but makes no comment on it. It stands as an unexplained detail. This reading from Hebrews explains the significance of the torn curtain. The Old Testament high priest entered the holy place once a year, on the Day of Atonement. Christ appeared in the fullness of time as the fulfillment of all that went before, "a high priest of the good things that have come." He is *the* high priest, "Fulfiller of the past/Promise of things to be," as Joseph Armitage Robinson wrote of him in the Transfiguration hymn "'Tis Good, Lord, to Be Here." He enters not an earthly tabernacle, tent, or even the temple in Jerusalem but the heavenly and eternal sanctuary on our behalf. He enters not year by year as did the high priest but "once for all." He entered not with the lifeblood of sacrificial animals but with his own human blood. As human sacrifice was rendered unnecessary by the introduction of animal sacrifice, so now animal sacrifice is rendered unnecessary by this divine-human sacrifice of the Son of God. What was achieved by this last and perpetually effective sacrifice was not a yearlong stay of divine judgment but a redemption that lasts forever. Like the Passover victim, he is a "lamb without blemish." The purpose of the sacrifice is to turn us from death to life, from selfish acting to the selfless service of God, from doing things for ourselves to worshiping God. Such is the revolutionary new covenant.

The epistle appointed in the *Book of Common Prayer* (**Heb. 11:39—12:3**) expands our understanding of this new covenant. The inclusiveness of this covenant reaches back into the past to embrace the believers who lived under the former covenant, the Hebrew saints. They did not receive the fullness of God's promises until Christ came. This was not to slight them because of when they were born. It was because of God's larger, more wonderful purpose, "since God had provided something better so that they would not, apart from us, be made perfect" (Heb. 11:40). Such were the "new things" that God had in store that have now been declared. And, we are reminded, if such better things were in store for those who lived under the old covenant, what wonderful new things does God have yet in store for us? How much larger is the whole people of God than we can yet know? We rejoice that the breadth of God's care expanded to include us. But surely that is not the limit to the circle of God's love and redemption. This week and the deeds it celebrates look not only backward. "Surrounded by so great a cloud of witnesses," we are not burdened by the past, weighed down by tradition, but we are lifted up, supported, exhilarated to run the race that is set before us, following the course blazed by Jesus who went through grief to joy, from shame to glory, from cross to crown. The collect the Prayer Book provides for this day prays:

> Almighty God, whose most dear Son went not up to joy but first he suffered pain, and entered not into glory before he was crucified: Mercifully grant

that we, walking in the way of the cross, may find it none other than the way of life and peace.

Such is the path we must all gladly follow. There is no other way to life and peace.

GOSPEL: JOHN 12:1-11; MARK 14:3-9

The Gospel for Monday in Holy Week, **John 12:1-11**, finds Jesus in "the home of Lazarus, whom he had raised from the dead." Filled with the serene confidence that characterizes John's portrait, Jesus goes boldly to Bethany, only two miles from Jerusalem, despite the plot against him. The previous chapter ended with the orders given by the chief priests and the Pharisees "that anyone who knew where Jesus was should let them know, so that they might arrest him" (11:57) for "they planned to put him to death" (11:53).

Lazarus prefigures Jesus' resurrection. Twice we are reminded that Lazarus is the one whom Jesus "had raised from the dead" (11:1, 9). Throughout this week, for all of its concentration on the passion, triumph is never far away. Indeed, if it were not for the knowledge of the resurrection, the crucifixion would not be the content of the church's proclamation. Christians can honor the crucifix only because they are sure of the conclusion of the story. So, in its paradoxical way, the crucifix is a proclamation of the resurrection, and the passion includes Easter.

The other event in this Gospel parallels the opening action of Mark's passion account, read yesterday on the Sunday of the Passion. The essentials are the same: a generous act of loving care prefigures the anointing of Jesus' corpse for burial. The actual anointing had to be deferred because when Jesus was taken down from the cross the Sabbath was about to begin; and when the women came Easter morning to do what they could not do before, they were again unable to do their work of embalming because they could not find the body. This anointing therefore takes on special significance.

The details in the two accounts, Mark and John, differ. In Mark the anointing takes place "in the house of Simon the leper"; in John, it occurs "in the home of Lazarus." In Mark the woman is nameless; in John she is Mary, the sister of Lazarus. In Mark, she anoints Jesus' head, as if he were a king; in John, she anoints his feet. In Mark, some malcontents mutter against her; in John it is Judas (for whom John has a clear hatred) who complains because he wants the money for himself. John ends his report of this event with the ominous words of Jesus, "You always have the poor with you, but you do not always have me." The dramatic words need no further comment as the shadows gather around the young prince of glory.

The alternative Gospel appointed in the *Book of Common Prayer* is a rereading of the passage concerning the anointing at Bethany read yesterday in Mark's passion. If one has chosen the option in the Prayer Book of reading just chapter 15 of Mark instead of Mark 14–15, this reading might be a wise choice. Moreover, since this is the year of Mark, this Gospel, **Mark 14:3-9**, might commend itself, since it parallels the Gospel from John appointed for this day in all four lectionaries.

Tuesday in Holy Week

Lectionary	First Lesson	Psalm	Second Lesson	Gospel
Revised Common	Isa. 49:1-7	Ps. 71:1-14	I Cor. 1:18-31	John 12:20-36
Episcopal (BCP)	Isa. 49:1-6	Ps. 71:1-12	I Cor. 1:18-31	John 12:37-38, 42-50 *or* Mark 11:15-19
Roman Catholic	Isa. 49:1-6			John 13:21-33, 36-38
Lutheran (LBW)	Isa. 49:1-6	Ps. 71:1-12	I Cor. 1:18-25	John 12:20-36

The Gospels have little concern for exact historical chronology, and so, while there have been attempts to assign various activities of Jesus to particular days of Holy Week, the actual events of Monday, Tuesday, and Wednesday remain uncertain. But that is no defect in Scripture or in liturgy. This week—as has already been seen—is not a chronological walking with Jesus from triumphal entry to crucifixion to burial to resurrection. It is rather an intense meditation on the meaning and significance of Jesus' passion and death. That meditation begins on the Sunday of the Passion and continues, with varying emphases, on each of the succeeding days of Holy Week.

FIRST LESSON: ISAIAH 49:1-7

The first lesson for Tuesday in Holy Week is the Second Servant Song, Isa. 49:1-6 (the Revised Common Lectionary extends the reading through v. 7). In the First Servant Song, read yesterday, God described the character of the chosen servant. Now in this second song the servant himself speaks. (The masculine pronoun is appropriate this week because of the association of the servant with Christ.)

The saga of this servant does not begin with his birth; it begins even before he was born. He is part of a long and continuing story: "The LORD called me before I was born." God in foreknowledge and according to sovereign plan is said also to have chosen the prophet Jeremiah before he was born (Jer. 1:5); Paul claims the same about himself (God "had set me apart before I was born and called me through his grace," Gal. 1:15). The point of the phrase "before I was born" is not to boast of special favor but just the opposite, reducing one who might claim a favored place to the status of servant of a plan already under way. Before they had accomplished anything, indeed before they were born, these few had been appointed their places in the history of salvation. In the fullest sense, that history reaches back through all the millennia of ancient Israel, back even before creation itself, to a time (although time had not yet begun) "before the foundation of the world" when God already knew what must be done to redeem the world. Christ, "the Lamb that was slaughtered from the foundation of the world" (Rev. 13:8), "was destined before the foundation of the world, but was revealed at the end of the ages" (1 Peter 1:20). God's foreknowledge includes even us, because to God all time is as the present. "He chose us in Christ before the foundation of the world to be holy and blameless" (Eph. 1:4).

Once again we learn that the strength of God is shown not in displays of naked power but rather in restraint. The servant is not given military weapons of destruction, but, the servant says, God "made my mouth like a sharp sword." The power is not of steel but of the far greater might of words. Then, having given the servant powerful speech, God did not turn him loose to display that power, but "in the shadow of his hand he hid me." The servant is made (like) an arrow, but, having been given this strength, "in his quiver he hid me away." The strength is hidden, kept in reserve for a time when it will be needed.

Those who seek to serve God faithfully know the frustration of that service: it seems to accomplish nothing. We have thought with the servant, "I have labored in vain, I have spent my strength for nothing and vanity." Hard and faithful work has gotten us nowhere. But, the servant teaches, it is not for us to judge success or failure. We need to learn to go on to the second half of the servant's complaint and to say with him, "Yet surely my cause is with the LORD, and my reward with my God." It is, we must learn, God's work and not ours, and that work will serve God's pleasure not as we might want but as God wants.

God's response to the complaint is not to give obvious success, not to make things go well, but to add still more responsibility. "It is too light a thing," God says with sarcasm, "that you should be my servant to raise up the tribes of Jacob and to restore the survivors of Israel." Is it too little to expect you to restore both kingdoms of ancient Israel? Here, then, is your additional job: "I will give you as a light to the nations that my salvation may reach to the end of the earth." The universal scope of God's concern is proclaimed once again. This week, we are reminded once more and continually, is not just for Christians, not just for Jews, but for all the world. Nothing less than the totality of humanity is to be our concern in response to such universal love.

SECOND LESSON: I CORINTHIANS 1:18-31

The second lesson (the epistle) in all but the Roman Catholic lectionary is 1 Cor. 1:18-31. The Roman Catholic lectionary, treating the first weekdays of Holy Week as ordinary weekdays are treated throughout the year, does not provide a second lesson for Monday, Tuesday, and Wednesday of Holy Week, providing only a reading from the Old Testament and a Gospel.

This week is given over entirely to the contemplation of the cross. If it was simply a matter of thinking about the ugly and cruel death of an innocent young man twenty centuries ago we would not need a week to do that. If we were simply to review the familiar details of the story, that could be done in less than half an hour of reading. But the Christian church gives an entire week to this concourse of events precisely because these events are not what they seem, for they reveal the way and the heart of God. For all the religious talk we hear around us and see on television, we have little understanding of sin and of God's way of dealing with it. This way, revealed this week, is filled with paradoxes and challenges to our way of thinking and acting. That is why we require a week of intense concentration and contemplation each year to begin to come to terms with this familiar yet disturbing story.

It is foolish to worship a dead man; it makes no earthly sense to adorn our altars with a cross or crucifix. It is like making an electric chair or a gas chamber the basic symbol of a religion. So it must seem to those outside, to those going the way of the world. "The message about the cross is foolishness to those who are perishing," Paul observed. Taking that road, going that direction, the cross and what it represents are senseless. But, Paul writes in this second lesson, to us who are going the other way, "who are being saved," the death of Christ is the very power of God. It is a matter of perspective.

The wisdom of the brightest people of the world is not the way to know God. If that were so that would limit the church to those with a high I.Q., and God has never promised to be logical or to make sense. "God decided, through the foolishness of our proclamation, to save those who believe." This faith is available to all, for it too is the gift of God. And those who receive it are in the process of being saved. Instantaneous conversion may happen to some like Paul, but for most of us it is a matter of continuing growth.

Notice the repetition in the concluding section of this reading (vv. 26-31): "Consider your call . . . God chose . . . God chose . . . God chose . . . He is the source of your life." The emphasis is not on our response but on God's initiative and God's call, and even faith is not our own doing. We are thrown entirely upon the mercy and the work of God in Christ. There our faith finds its focus and its source.

GOSPEL: JOHN 12:20-36; 13:21-33, 36-38, 42-50; MARK 11:15-19

The paradoxes of God's dealing with us are evident in the Gospel appointed in the *Lutheran Book of Worship* and the Revised Common Lectionary, **John 12:20-36**. Dying yields life; "those who love their life lose it, and those who hate their life in this world will keep it for eternal life"; Jesus' "hour" is the time of his passion and death, and that death is his glorification.

Throughout the Gospel story, even as in John's account the circle of faithful believers is becoming smaller and smaller, people keep breaking in from the outside. In this Gospel some Gentiles ("Greeks") come to Philip and ask to see Jesus. Very little in the Gospel story is to be taken at face value, and so when these Gentiles ask to "see" Jesus, they mean to do more than just look him over, shake his hand, get an autograph. Here, seeing is close to believing. Their desire to "see" is an earnest seeking of the one who was to draw all people to himself. "We wish to see Jesus": That request prepares for Jesus' announcement, "The hour has come for the Son of Man to be glorified." What the Greeks were to see was the victorious death of the Son of Man. Jesus then adds the sobering comment, "Whoever serves me must follow me" into death and thus into honored glory.

The death of Jesus, that from the point of view of the world ought to repel those who must look at it, in fact draws people—not just the curious but all people—to him. The crucifix shines like a beacon, giving light to the world (cf. the first lesson: "I will give you as a light to the nations") so that those who believe may be enlightened with the knowledge of God.

The Gospel appointed in the *Book of Common Prayer*, **John 12:37-38, 42-50**, deals with the same themes of darkness versus light, unbelief versus belief, human glory versus "the glory that comes from God." The final paragraph (vv. 44-50) describes the relationship between Jesus and the Father. Jesus is the perfectly obedient servant and child of God, for God's commandment "is eternal life." The identities of the two overlap. Whoever sees and believes in Jesus sees and believes in God. Throughout this section the stress falls on the goodness and the graciousness of God; "I came not to judge the world but to save the world."

The alternative Gospel provided in the Prayer Book, **Mark 11:15-19**, may commend itself this year of Mark. It describes Jesus' cleansing of the temple, which Mark seems to place on Monday in Holy Week. Mark's peculiar emphasis is seen in v. 16, absent in Matthew's and Luke's accounts, "He would not allow anyone to carry anything through the temple." Jesus, in strict adherence to the law, is consumed by a passion for the holiness of the temple and the rites that were performed there. The temple precincts were not to be used as a thoroughfare, and secular work was not to be done in the holy place. Moreover, Mark expands the ancient words, quoted by Matthew and Luke, "My house shall be called a house of prayer," to include "for all the nations" (Isa. 56:7). Jesus was purifying the holy place not just for Jews but for all. Jerusalem is to be the focus of the whole world, and its holy place to be universally reverenced.

The cleansing of the temple is to be understood as a dramatic explication of the meaning of the cursing of the fig tree, which precedes the cleansing of the temple, and the withered fig tree that follows. The tree shows the fate of Jerusalem and a religion that abounds in show (leaves) but bears little fruit. Judgment and cleansing are inevitable and are what the crucifixion are all about. (For what may be a rejection of the centrality of Jerusalem and its replacement by Galilee, see the Gospel for the Easter Vigil, below.)

Jesus' action increased his opponents' desire to kill him, but they were intimidated by the admiration the crowds had for him. So they watched and waited. The suspense builds.

(The Gospel appointed in the Roman Catholic lectionary, John 13:21-33, 36-38, is treated below in connection with Wednesday in Holy Week.)

Wednesday in Holy Week

Lectionary	First Lesson	Psalm	Second Lesson	Gospel
Revised Common	Isa. 50:4-9a	Psalm 70	Heb. 12:1-3	John 13:21-32
Episcopal (BCP)	Isa. 50:4-9a	Ps. 69:7-15, 22-23	Heb. 9:11-15, 24-28	John 13:21-35 or Matt. 26:1-5, 14-25
Roman Catholic	Isa. 50:4-9a			Matt. 26:14-25
Lutheran (LBW)	Isa. 50:4-9a	Ps. 70:1-2, 4-6	Rom. 5:6-11	Matt. 26:14-25

On Wednesday in Holy Week, according to the Synoptic chronology, Judas "went to the chief priests in order to betray" Jesus to them and receive their promise of money (Mark 14:10-12; also Matt. 26:14-16; Luke 22:3-6). So, because Judas became a clandestine agent for the governing authorities, Wednesday in Holy Week became known as "Spy Wednesday." The tradition that gave rise to the nickname is preserved in the Gospel appointed for this day in the *Lutheran Book of Worship* and in the Roman Catholic lectionary and in the alternative Gospel appointed in the *Book of Common Prayer*. It is alluded to less clearly in the Gospel appointed in the *Book of Common Prayer* and in the Revised Common Lectionary.

FIRST LESSON: ISAIAH 50:4-9

The first lesson is from the Third Servant Song, Isa. 50:4-9a (the First Servant Song was heard on Monday, the Second on Tuesday), a repetition of the verses read in the Revised Common Lectionary and in part (vv. 4-7) in the Roman Catholic lectionary on the Sunday of the Passion.

The servant speaks as God's agent to console and encourage Israel. He brings this consolation by sacrificial suffering, giving his back to those who would beat him, his cheeks "to those who pulled out the beard," his face to insult and spitting. This submissive reaction to their hostility comes not from weakness or an unwillingness to resist their rude violence but, paradoxically, as we are learning this week, from his confidence in God's help and in God's strength because of God's sure vindication. His serene confidence is rooted in God's certain care.

The servant is an obedient listener who is therefore able to teach his people, "to sustain the weary with a word." His instruction, like his strength, is not his but flows through him from God, who opens the ear and teaches and supports and vindicates. Thus the servant can take on any and all comers, confident of triumph.

SECOND LESSON: ROMANS 5:6-11; HEBREWS 9:11-15, 24-28; 12:1-3

The second lesson differs in each of the three lectionaries. (The Roman Catholic lectionary does not provide a second lesson for Monday, Tuesday, or Wednesday.)

The *Lutheran Book of Worship* appoints **Rom. 5:6-11**. In this memorable passage Paul sets forth the consequences of the redemptive death of Christ. It is an extension of the idea in the first lesson: as God has dealt with the servant, so the Servant-Son has dealt with us. "God proves his love for us in that while we still were sinners Christ died for us" (5:8). Thus made righteous by the past deed, we look forward in confidence to the future: we will "be saved through him from the wrath of God" (v. 9). Such is the transforming work of God, who has made enemies friends and who by death gives life. By the *past* deed we have been reconciled to God. For the *future* we have the assurance of deliverance from the final judgment. *Now* in the present we, like the suffering servant to whom we now belong and who lives in us, can taunt our enemies, confident in God's love and strength.

The epistle (second lesson) appointed in the *Book of Common Prayer*, **Heb. 9:11-15, 24-28**, explains in terms of the sacrifices of ancient Israel how Christ as both priest and victim accomplished the redemption of the world. The passage is discussed above in connection with the appointments in the Lutheran lectionary and the Revised Common Lectionary for Monday in Holy Week. This sacrifice by and of the eternal high priest removes the penalty of sin (v. 26). For mortals death is inevitable and then after it comes the judgment. For Christ death occurred once on behalf of many, and later he will appear not as wrathful judge but as the long-awaited Savior, "to save those who are eagerly waiting for him" (v. 28).

The Revised Common Lectionary appoints **Heb. 12:1-3**, part of the *BCP* epistle for Monday in Holy Week (see above). We are surrounded by a great cloud of witnesses—the heroes listed in chap. 11 (Abel, Enoch, Noah, Abraham, Sarah, Isaac, Jacob and Esau, Joseph, Moses, Gideon, Barak, Samson, Jephthah, David, Samuel and the prophets, and all the host of unnamed faithful "of whom the world was not worthy" [11:38]). With such a company surrounding us and with Jesus going ahead as the "pioneer and perfecter of our faith" we run the course that is set before us. The certainty of future and eternal joy enables us, like Christ, to endure shame, suffering, and even death. The assurance of his reign, even now, "at the right hand of the throne of God" (12:3), gives us hope and confidence.

GOSPEL: MATTHEW 26:14-25; JOHN 13:21-25

The Lutheran, Roman Catholic and the alternative Episcopal Gospel reading is the key to the chronological commemoration of Wednesday in Holy Week—Judas' betrayal of Jesus in **Matt. 26:14-25**. Judas went on his own; he was not seduced by the chief priests. Greed seems to have been his motive, as it so often is with those in our own time who betray their country. As Matthew tells it, Judas asked them bluntly, "What is betrayal worth?" Matthew explicitly says that they paid him and also specifies the amount—thirty pieces of silver. That detail is in keeping with Matthew's interest in the fulfillment of Old Testament passages. Here he seems to have in mind Zech. 11:12, the price of a slave (Exod. 21:32). Mark and Luke, it is interesting to note, do not report any payment to Judas. On the strength of a promise of money Judas "began to look for an opportunity to betray" Jesus (Mark 14:11; Luke 22:6). Judas' offer facilitates the leaders' desire to get rid of Jesus. They had planned to arrest him "by stealth and kill him," but after the Passover was completed (Matt. 26:45). Judas' betrayal of Jesus—the horror that "one of the twelve" (we are constantly reminded of his membership in the apostolic band) would dare to do this runs through the passion account—makes it possible for the chief priests and elders to carry out their plan earlier than they had expected. The conspirators' good fortune appears to doom Jesus, but it is part of a larger purpose that will ultimately overturn their plot, but not until Jesus is dead and buried.

The traitorous character of Judas was no surprise to Jesus. At the Passover meal, which we know as the last supper, while they were eating the paschal lamb, Jesus announced, "One of you will betray me" (v. 21). With the quiet assurance of the suffering servant of the first lesson, Jesus is confident that what he is about to do is in accordance with the Scriptures: "The Son of Man goes as it is written of him" (26:24). But he condemns the one who brings it about with the devastating judgment, "It would have been better for that one not to have been born." Judas has the cool effrontery to ask, "Surely not I?" Jesus' answer is not as evasive as it appears. "You have said so." With the confession not far from Judas' lips and with Jesus' confirmation, the reading ends. The impact is nearly overwhelming.

The Gospel appointed for this day by the *Book of Common Prayer* (**John 13:21-35**) and by the Revised Common Lectionary (**John 13:21-32**) and the Roman Catholic Gospel for Tuesday in Holy Week presents John's picture of the last supper. There is no narrative of the institution of the Lord's Supper. Instead John describes a kind of anti-communion by intinction. Jesus gives Judas a piece of bread dipped in the dish, and when Judas receives it, Satan enters him. Instead of the divine, this bread communicates the diabolical; instead of life it conveys death; instead of forgiveness, condemnation. Judas is dismissed from the table not with "Go in peace to love and serve the Lord" but with the stern command, "Do quickly what you are going to do." The remaining eleven in their characteristic misunderstanding and obtuseness assumed that Judas was being told to give something to the poor—Judas of whom we heard it said on Monday that he did not care about the poor and "was a thief" (John 12:6). Judas, who for greed had betrayed Jesus, was not about to give away money to the poor. With the bread of condemnation in his mouth and with Jesus' words ringing in his ears, Judas immediately leaves. John concludes the incident with the dramatic observation, "It was night" (v. 30). Early in the Gospel Nicodemus symbolically came out of the darkness to Jesus the light of the world. Now as the Gospel draws to a close Judas turns his back on the light and slips out into the darkness.

Then, with the betrayer gone, having taken the shadows with him, Jesus can announce with added impact, "Now the Son of Man has been glorified and God has been glorified in him" (v. 31). The gospel of glory approaches its climax, and the radiance of the Light begins to penetrate and dispel the darkness.

Jesus is soon to leave their sight, and his visible presence will soon be gone. Yet he will not be gone, for as testimony to him the disciples are to "love one another." They are to reflect and reveal the intimate love between the Father and the Son, and in that love Christ will remain in, with, and among his people.

The Roman Catholic Gospel for Tuesday in Holy Week includes these verses (21-32) and adds vv. 36-38. The betrayal by Judas finds an unwelcome echo in the weakness of Peter. For all his brave words, Peter will this night deny not once but three times that he even knows Jesus.

Maundy Thursday/Holy Thursday

Lectionary	First Lesson	Psalm	Second Lesson	Gospel
Revised Common	Exod. 12:1-4 (5-10), 11-14	Ps. 116:1-2, 12-19	1 Cor. 11:23-26	John 13:1-17, 31b-35
Episcopal (BCP)	Exod. 12:1-14a	Ps. 78:14-20, 23-25	1 Cor. 11:23-26 (27-32)	John 13:1-15 *or* Luke 22:14-30
Roman Catholic	Exod. 12:1-8, 11-14a	Ps. 116:10, 12-13, 15-18	1 Cor. 11:23-26	John 13:1-15
Lutheran (LBW)	Exod. 24:3-11	Ps. 116:10-17	1 Cor. 10:16-17 (18-21)	Mark 14:12-26

With the evening service on this day, the Triduum (one day made of three) begins, the climax of this week and the central celebration of the entire church year. These are the high holy days of Christianity. In these three days the essence of the proclamation of Christianity is distilled in the swiftly moving, dramatic events: supper, arrest, trial, crucifixion, burial, resurrection. Since Advent everything has been moving toward this "hour"; the remainder of the church year flows from these events. The cross and resurrection stand at the center of the year and of all time.

The *Book of Common Prayer* as well as the Roman Catholic and Revised Common lectionaries all appoint a common set of lessons for Maundy Thursday to serve all three years of the lectionary cycle. The *Lutheran Book of Worship* alone provides three sets, one for each of the three years.

FIRST LESSON: EXODUS 12:1-14; 24:3-11

The first lesson in the *Book of Common Prayer* and the Roman Catholic and Revised Common lectionaries (and in the *Lutheran Book of Worship* for Year A) presents the institution of the Passover in **Exod. 12:1-14**, the perpetual memorial of the Lord's deliverance of the people of Israel from slavery. The historical context and details are interesting but largely tangential to the use of this reading in Christian churches this evening: the nomadic origins, the relation to the first full moon of the spring, the postexilic calendar that made this festival mark the beginning of the year, the assumption of a highly organized "congregation of Israel" in Egypt, the requirement of roasting not boiling the lamb for the meal, the careful disposal of what remains. Easter often but not always is celebrated near the time when the Jews celebrate Passover, and the relationship between the

Jewish Passover and the Christian version of the festival ("Christ our Passover is sacrificed for us," 1 Cor. 5:7) needs to be respectfully examined by Christians as two ways of celebrating one festival.

In the context of Maundy Thursday, however, other concerns commend themselves to the preacher. The emphasis of the readings is not on the Holy Communion as the Christian Passover meal but on the whole act of deliverance from slavery and death. As "Palm Sunday" is far more than a commemoration of the triumphal entry of Jesus into Jerusalem and is most of all the Sunday of the Passion presenting the story that is the subject of the contemplation this entire week, so Maundy Thursday is more than a commemoration of the "birthday of the chalice" (an early name for the day) and is rather an introduction to and preview of the events that follow—the Triduum. The Lamb is Christ, proclaimed as the Lamb of God; he is "a lamb without blemish," a young male, whose blood protects his people from death. Luther's Easter hymn, "Christ Jesus Lay in Death's Strong Bands," sings of Christ,

> See, his blood now marks our door;
> Faith points to it; death passes o'er,
> And Satan cannot harm us.

As the ancient Hebrews ate the lamb in an evening meal, so Christians eat the Lamb in the evening meal of the Lord's Supper. The meal is eaten in readiness for the march, by people prepared to move out on a perilous but liberating journey from security to risk and on to final safety, going into the wilderness but at last to the promised land beyond.

The *Lutheran Book of Worship* appoints for this Year B of the lectionary cycle **Exod. 24:3-11**, a lesson that points to the celebration of the Holy Communion. Moses and the elders of Israel "beheld God, and they ate and drank" (v. 11). Sharing a meal in the presence of God, they discover the presence of God in the act of eating and drinking. The meal ratified the covenant as Moses and the elders shared the meal as representatives of Israel. Another version of the ratification of the covenant, inserted into this story, emphasizes the participation of all the people in the ratification process. It is the odd and, to modern taste, repellent story of Moses, the mediator of the covenant, splashing half the blood of the oxen and other sacrificial animals on the altar and the other half of the blood on the people. The splashing of blood showed how seriously this covenant—the Ten Commandments and the laws of the covenant—were to be taken. Life was taken so that the law might live; and the law, if obeyed, had the power to give life. The Christian Eucharist, which proclaims "the death of the Lord until he comes," is a still more profound presentation of the same truth: life was given in exchange for life. That transaction lays the responsibility of a new and obedient life on those whose lives have been purchased by the life of another.

SECOND LESSON: I CORINTHIANS 11:23-32; 10:16-17

The second lesson in the *Book of Common Prayer*, Roman Catholic, and Revised Common lectionaries (and in the *Lutheran Book of Worship* in Year A as an alternative), **1 Cor. 11:23-32**, is Paul's account of the institution of the Lord's Supper. The tradition regarding the Supper is unbroken, passed from the Lord himself to the apostles to Paul who now passes it on to the Corinthians and to those, including us, who read his letter to them. Those who receive the tradition keep it alive not just by telling the story but by doing what it commands: "Do this in remembrance of me" (vv. 24, 25). For, Paul comments, "as often as you eat this bread and drink the cup, you proclaim the Lord's death until he comes" (v. 26). Such eating and drinking is itself a proclamation. The meal takes on a special significance when it is celebrated this night. It participates in the events being celebrated—the death and resurrection of Christ, who is priest and victim. The bread is identified with his body, the cup with his blood; broken and poured out they prefigure, anticipate, and proclaim the sacrifice on the cross, making it available in an intimate and personal way to believers of all times and all places. In this meal we who live two millennia after the events and in a vastly changed world have our share in those saving events. The blood of sacrificial animals that ratified the first covenant is here replaced by the blood of the sinless Son of God to ratify the new covenant.

The meal is celebrated "in remembrance of me." This sacramental meal is no pale memorial or mere reminder of long-past events. In the Bible, to "remember" is to keep alive in such a vivid and vital way that the separation in time between then and now and the separation in space between there and here are erased. The past is brought into the present. History lives still, and we and the apostles become contemporaries. Such is the power of ritual, as all ancient people have recognized.

The *Book of Common Prayer* provides the option of extending the reading through v. 32. The solemn warning Paul gives the Corinthians enriches our understanding of the Holy Supper. The setting of Paul's report of the institution of the Supper is his condemnation of the behavior of the Corinthian Christians at the table of the Eucharist. It was their custom to celebrate the Eucharist during an *agape* meal, but instead of being a "love feast," as *agape* implies, the meal became the occasion for factional quarrels and general selfishness. "When the time comes to eat, each of you goes ahead with your own supper, and one goes hungry and another becomes drunk!" Thus they "show contempt for the church of God and humiliate those who have nothing" (vv. 21-22). Paul's response to this deplorable behavior is first to remind them of Christ's institution of the Holy Supper and secondly to explain to them the ties that bind together those who share the Supper with one another. The celebration of the crucifixion is for Paul a communal action. Those who eat and drink this communion "in an unworthy manner will be answerable for the body and blood of the Lord." This is not just bread and wine they are consuming; Jesus Christ, the crucified Savior, is present in the meal. Those who partake of the meal ought therefore to examine themselves in preparation. Traditionally this has meant some form of examination of conscience and confession, cleansing oneself before sharing in the Supper.

But there is a further dimension that requires understanding. "For all who eat and drink without discerning the body, eat and drink judgment against themselves." One interpretation of that passage (common among Lutherans) has stressed the recognition of the Real Presence: unwittingly taking the true body and blood of Christ into an unprepared body is dangerous, even fatal. The holy God is present in this meal, and "it is a fearful thing to fall into the hands of the living God," the writer to the Hebrews warns (Heb. 10:31). But in the context of this passage "the body" seems to refer not to the reception of the body of Christ in communion (no mention is made in this verse of the blood). Rather, "the body" seems to refer to the presence of the body of church, the community that is the body of Christ. When we receive the Holy Communion we are communing not only with Christ but also with all believers of all times and all places. We eat and drink with Christ and with the church. Those who do not discern this communal dimension and act as if the sacrament is only an individual matter between Christ and them bring judgment upon themselves for ignoring those around them. In their self-centeredness they do not notice the needs of others.

The *Lutheran Book of Worship* appoints as the second lesson **1 Cor. 10:16-17**. This brief pericope stresses the intimacy of the presence of Christ in the Supper and the unity of all who share in the sacred meal. The context concerns religious meals eaten in the presence of idols: Christians are not to participate in pagan worship. But these two verses that comprise the reading stand alone as they are read and heard this night. They assert by means of a rhetorical question the presence of Christ in the Supper. This meal is to be taken therefore with utmost seriousness; it must never be a trivial affair.

GOSPEL: JOHN 13:1-7, 31b-35; MARK 14:12-16; LUKE 22:14-30

Maundy Thursday derives its name from the Gospel appointed in the *Book of Common Prayer*, Roman Catholic, and Revised Common lectionaries, the new commandment (*mandatum* in Latin) to love one another. It has been the Gospel appointed for this day at least since the early middle ages.

In obediently acting out the command in this Gospel to "wash one another's feet," the church used John 13:34 as an antiphon with the foot washing (in Latin, of course: *mandatum novum do vobis*, "A new commandment I give you"—love one another).

This Gospel may be understood as the beginning of John's narrative of the passion. This reading begins with the announcement, "his hour had come to depart from this world and go to the Father" (13:1). A lengthy section of discourse, 13:18—16:33, and the "high priestly prayer" in chap. 17, are inserted into the action of the narrative, not only building suspense but explaining, before the events of the "hour" occur, what they mean so that we can understand the depth of their significance as we watch them unfold. This a reversal of the previous pattern of John's Gospel. Up until now the pattern has been a dramatic action or "sign" followed by a discourse by Jesus explaining the significance of the action. Now with what may be regarded as the last and greatest of the "signs," the discourse prepares us to watch the crucifixion and see (in the Johannine sense, to believe) what is happening.

John departs from the Synoptic account of the last supper in two significant but related ways. In John there is no narrative of the institution of the Lord's Supper. Perhaps, many suggest, the miraculous feeding of the five thousand and the resulting discourse, reported in John 6 with unmistakable eucharistic overtones, serve as John's way of explaining the meaning of the Holy Communion, relating it to the manna that sustained the Hebrews in the wilderness. John's second departure from the Synoptic account of the last supper is that John, instead of the institution narrative, provides an action that is not reported in the Synoptics or in Paul: Jesus' washing of the disciples' feet. This substitution may be John's way of presenting what is otherwise shown and conveyed in the Eucharist. Massey Shepherd has suggested in *The Oxford American Prayer Book Commentary* that the action of humble and loving service by Jesus himself may be given by John as a compelling example of the kind of love of which the Holy Communion is the supreme memorial and of the grace and love that the Eucharist was intended to nourish in the lives of those who claim Jesus as "Teacher and Lord."

The various readings for Holy Week come to a focus in this Gospel. The Gospel for Monday in Holy Week shows Mary of Bethany anointing Jesus' feet with costly perfume in a demonstration by this woman of the extravagant self-giving love that Jesus was soon to show on the cross. Now, as the Triduum begins, it is Jesus himself who washes his disciples' feet. It is not only an intensification of Mary's action; it is a dramatic portrayal of the *kenosis* described in the second lesson (epistle) for Passion Sunday, Phil. 2:5-11, the self-emptying of "Christ Jesus who . . . emptied himself, taking the form of a slave," who poured himself out, as the Greek word implies, as his lifeblood drained from him. Christ removes his outer robe, as he laid aside his preexistent glory, and "tied a towel around himself," taking the role of a slave. He "poured water into a basin," and careful readers will recall the significance of water in the Fourth Gospel as a sign of the life-giving Holy Spirit.

Peter, impulsive and this time understandably imperceptive, flatly refuses to let his Teacher and Lord wash his feet. He refuses out of his love and obedience to Jesus, saying in effect, "*You* will never wash my feet; you are the Lord, I am the servant. I cannot let you demean yourself." Jesus' stern warning, "Unless I wash you, you have no share with me," demolishes Peter's rejection. The fear of being cut off from Jesus makes Peter demand in his exaggerated way, wildly swinging from one extreme to the other, "Lord, not my feet only but also my hands and my head," as if to say, "I want to be wholly yours." As Peter had said earlier, "Lord, to whom can we go? You have the words of eternal life" (John 6:68). He alone is the Holy One, he alone is the Lord, he alone is the Most High, apart from whom there is no life, no hope.

Jesus, having washed their feet, put his robe back on and resumed his place at the table. In a small space he symbolically foreshows the resumption of his power and glory at the throne of God when the crucifixion was completed and his earthly work done. (John, it should be recalled, does not separate into distinct events the resurrection, the ascension, and the gift of the Holy Spirit.)

He then charges his disciples to do as he has done to them. Many Christian churches are recovering a literal obedience to the command, "You also ought to wash one another's feet." It is more than practicing an outward

PREPARED BY

DATE

PAGE
NO.

executive®

ceremony. The foot washing is a sign of service. If Jesus has served us in such self-giving love, so we ought to serve one another. We are to show in the way we treat one another the love that we have received. In medieval rites being recovered in many places today, the meaning of the foot washing was explained in a series of anthems sung while it was taking place. The first of these was John 13:34, "A new commandment I give you, that you love one another." The Revised Common Lectionary includes these verses (31b-35) in the Gospel reading to supply the interpretation and the application of the foot washing: "By this everyone will know that you are my disciples, if you have love for one another."

The Gospel appointed by the *Lutheran Book of Worship* for Year B, **Mark 14:12-26**, is a repetition of the passage from the Passion according to Mark read this year on the Sunday of the Passion, concerning the institution of the Lord's Supper. It lays the foundation for what will be done later this evening in the celebration of the Eucharist, the perpetual memorial of the death of Christ. In this reading Jesus is in command. Nothing takes him by surprise. He knows apparently by supernatural insight what the two disciples he sends into Jerusalem will find and what the arrangements for their Passover meal will be. He knows about Judas' planned betrayal and freely accepts it; the Passover lamb willingly is sacrificed. The whole course of events is unfolding "according to the definite plan and foreknowledge of God" (Acts 2:23).

The *Book of Common Prayer* offers as an alternative Gospel **Luke 22:14-30**. This reading joins the institution narrative with the command to follow Jesus' example of service of one another. Judas' betrayal is condemned, but the eleven are not to be commended here. At the very table of the first Eucharist they argue about which of them was to be regarded as the greatest. Jesus declares that concern to be not only unworthy but wrongheaded. They have not yet understood the meaning of Jesus' "perfect life of love" and loving service of others. Those who share this meal are thus intimately bound to Christ who lives in and through them, and they are therefore obliged to live the new life "as one who serves."

The Maundy Thursday liturgy does not (or should not) come to a clear close, for it is but the first part of a unitive three-day service proclaiming the act that worked our salvation, the death and resurrection of Christ. Liturgical churches allow the principal service of this evening to decline into darkness.

The desolation is deepened in many churches by the stripping of the altar. The candles are extinguished; the vessels and ornaments, altar cloths and hangings are removed; and the sanctuary is left desolate, stark, and bare. It is a powerful representation of the desertion of Christ by his disciples. So he is left to face crucifixion utterly alone. In the chilling words of John's Gospel, "And it was night."

In various churches, the solemnity is prolonged by a prayerful watch, a practice traceable to the fourth century. This watch in the church recalls and is kept in union with Christ's watch and prayer in Gethsemane. In some places the watch is kept before the altar of repose where the consecrated bread and wine are kept until the communion on Good Friday.

Thus this evening Eucharist marks the beginning of an extended service that continues until the dawn of Easter morning. As with Judaism still, the evening is the beginning of the day, and so the events of Maundy Thursday are united with the death of Christ the next afternoon and the hasty burial. Then, "when the sabbath was past," there is a stirring in the darkness of the tomb.

Good Friday

Lectionary	First Lesson	Psalm	Second Lesson	Gospel
Revised Common	Isa. 52:13—53:12	Psalm 22	Heb. 10:16-25 *or* Heb. 4:14-16; 5:7-9	John 18:1—19:42
Episcopal (BCP)	Isa. 52:13—53:12 *or* Gen. 22:1-18 *or* Wisd. 2:1, 12-24	Ps. 22:1-21 *or* 22:1-11 *or* 40:1-14 *or* 69:1-23	Heb. 10:1-25	John (18:1-40) 19:1-37
Roman Catholic	Isa. 52:13—53:12	Ps. 31:2, 6, 12-13, 15-17, 25	Heb. 4:14-16; 5:7-9	John 18:1—19:42
Lutheran (LBW)	Isa. 52:13—53:12 *or* Hosea 6:1-6	Ps. 22:1-23	Heb. 4:14-16; 5:7-9	John 18:1—19:42 *or* John 19:17-30

This most solemn day began, in the Jewish and early Christian reckoning, with sundown on Maundy Thursday. It is therefore to be understood as a continuation of the three-day celebration begun at the last supper. The central theme of the day is the cross, a word that in the New Testament reverberates with rich and manifold meaning. It is the instrument of death of Christ as well as the death itself, but the cross also speaks of sacrifice and self-giving love and perfect obedience, redemption and atonement. The cross also speaks of victory, for the cross includes the resurrection, indeed would be robbed of meaning without it. The cross is the essential content of the message of Christian preaching (1 Cor. 1:17-18), and it stands at the heart of the Christian story (Gal. 6:12, 14). The complex meanings—death and life, defeat and victory—are perhaps no more compellingly set forth than in the passion according to John, which since ancient times has been appointed as the Gospel for Good Friday.

FIRST LESSON: ISAIAH 52:13—53:12; GENESIS 22:1-18; WISDOM 2:1, 12-24

The first lesson in all four lectionaries is the Fourth Servant Song, **Isa. 52:13—53:12**. (The First Servant Song was read on Monday, the Second on Tuesday, the Third on Wednesday and also in the Roman Catholic and Revised Common lectionaries on the Sunday of the Passion.) This Fourth Song is not only next in order in Isaiah, but it is the one that most explicitly makes Christians think in terms of the passion of Christ. If we did not know the context, we might perhaps think that we were hearing an eyewitness account of the crucifixion: "despised," "rejected," "wounded," "cut off from the land of the living," "numbered among the transgressors." The interpretation of this suffering sounds like familiar Christian language. "He was wounded for our transgressions . . . upon him was the punishment that made us whole, and by his bruises we are healed."

The responsible preacher, however, must do more than simply point out the striking parallels. Literalists may want to say that Isaiah looked into the future and accurately and in detail saw the suffering of the Messiah. Others will explain the parallels by saying that Jesus the Jew gathered into himself the suffering of his people and took his people's experience as his own. Still others will say that the accounts of the passion were written with an eye on the Hebrew Bible and were shaped at least in part so that they would seem to fulfill ancient words and present a seamless history of unmistakable significance. In any case, the meaning of the Hebrew text is not as certain as we might like to think, and translations and interpretations must rest upon a degree of conjecture.

There is exaggeration in the text that makes us hesitate in applying it directly and easily to Jesus. His appearance was marred "beyond human semblance, and his form beyond that of mortals" (52:14). In even the most vivid and gruesome portrayal of the passion and death (one may think of baroque Italian and Spanish crucifixes), Jesus is recognizable as a human being. Indeed it is that very humanity that commands our attention. Beaten and bloody, exhausted by his ordeal, he is most clearly one of us, and our hearts go out to him as to any victim of brutality and violence.

"It was the will of the LORD to crush him" (53:10). There can be no more abhorrent portrayal of the character of God than that: a sadistic monster who wanted to destroy his fragile and obedient servant-son. It will not do, therefore, to take every verse and bend it to point toward Christ in his passion. It is important, however, to notice the clear progression in this passage from suffering to reward, from affliction to promise. The movement recalls that of Psalm 22, which begins in desolation, "My God, why have you forsaken me?" (as in Mark's passion account read this past Sunday), but ends in confidence, moving from lament to praise.

The first section of the lesson (52:13—53:3) describes the disfigurement of the servant, so astonishing to earthly rulers that they could say nothing in his presence, and his rejection by everyone.

The second section (53:4-9) explains that the suffering was on our behalf. "He was stricken for the transgression of my people" (v. 8). His wounds heal us, and his brokenness makes us whole.

But the final section (53:10-12) speaks of the servant's future, for despite the intensity of his suffering, he will not die. Indeed, "he shall see his offspring, and shall prolong his days." "Out of his anguish he shall see light . . . therefore I will allot him a portion with the great."

The opening and closing verses are of particular interest. The song opens with a promise before it descends into the depths of suffering: "See, my servant shall prosper; he shall be exalted and lifted up, and shall be very high" (52:13). The song concludes with a somber reminder of the cost and the purpose of his sacrifice: he will rejoice with the great and the strong "because he poured out himself to death, and was numbered with the transgressors." When Christ came to us to suffer for us the outcome was sure, and when he returned to his heavenly place he took with him the wounds he eternally bears in his body. His pain, as well as ours, is not forgotten or buried in the past or erased. It is transformed and given purpose and meaning.

The *Book of Common Prayer* provides two other options for the First Lesson. **Genesis 22:1-18**, Abraham's sacrifice of Isaac, is treated below in connection with the Easter Vigil for which it is appointed in all four lectionaries. The other option, **Wisd. 2:1, 12-24**, presents the reasoning of the "ungodly" (Wisd. 1:16). The point of view of such apparently realistic people is that death is the unavoidable and irreversible end of each life. "No one has been known to return" once one departs to Hades, the place of the dead. Before the preacher too quickly dismisses such a view, its reasonableness as far as many in the world are concerned ought to be acknowledged if the power of the resurrection is to be proclaimed. If it were not for the power of God shown in Christ, what the ungodly say is accurate. Regarding the crucifixion from another point of view, that of an unbeliever, may be a helpful approach, if that point of view is represented fairly and honestly. This is not as easy to do as it may seem.

Verses 12-24 present the attitude of these children of this world toward the righteous man, who on Good Friday is easily identified with Christ. Why was there such hostility toward Jesus? These verses lay it out clearly: "He is inconvenient to us and opposes our actions" (2:12). Christ was and still is crucified because he accuses us, makes us uncomfortable with the way we are living our lives. So "the very sight of him is a burden to us, because his manner of life is unlike that of others, and his ways are strange" (v. 15). He intensifies this difference for us "by professing to have knowledge of God"; "he boasts that God is his Father" (vv. 13, 15).

The responsible approach to these lessons for Good Friday is to put the blame where it belongs—on each of us. Preachers easily—too easily—point the finger at the outrageous lives of rock stars and television personalities and politicians, and Christians have from time to time laid the blame for the death of Jesus upon the Romans or the Jews. But as we hear these lessons for today these actors in the drama who oppose Jesus stand for us and our quieter but no less obstinate rebellion and our callous rejection of

God's claim on us. We are to recognize and acknowledge our role in cruci-
fying the Son of God, in making this sacrificial death necessary. In a devastating admission, Johann Heermann's hymn "Ah, Holy Jesus" has us
sing, "I crucified thee."

The taunts heaped upon the righteous servant echo more in the passion
accounts of Matthew and Mark ("Let us see if his words are true . . . let us
test him") than in today's Gospel. Those who reason in this way do so
because of their limited vision. They cannot see far enough or wait long
enough. For "the secret purposes of God" include death. This death of the
Righteous One is in fact the clearest revelation of the will and the character
of God, overturning "the devil's envy," conquering hostility by submitting
to it, and trampling down death by death.

SECOND LESSON: HEBREWS 4:14-16; 5:7-9; 10:1-25

Good Friday is not a day of desolation and defeat. Through it and from it
flows a stream of life and triumph. The second lesson in the Lutheran and
Roman Catholic lectionaries and the alternative lesson in the Revised
Common Lectionary, **Heb. 4:14-16; 5:7-9**, is suffused with hope and confidence and is thus an effective preparation for hearing John's passion.
Jesus is the living high priest, the minister of grace and mercy, the source
of eternal salvation. As the high priest under the old covenant passed each
year at Passover through the veil of the temple in Jerusalem into the holiest
place, so Jesus, our high priest, has done in fact what the preceding high
priests had done symbolically; he has passed into the heavens, the holiest
place where God dwells. Already, even on Good Friday, we glimpse the
ascension. Indeed, we can celebrate Good Friday only because Jesus "has
passed through the heavens." Our high priest is like us, tested as we are,
and knows our life because he lived it, enduring the temptations that surround us. There is, however, one significant difference: he has resisted the
temptation and is without sin. He lived the perfect life that is expected of
us, and he did it in our stead and on our behalf.

"In the days of his flesh, Jesus offered up prayers and supplications,
with loud cries and tears" (5:7). The reference is more specific than the
general prayer life of Jesus, his continual prayer throughout his life. The
writer to the Hebrews, like us who hear this reading on Good Friday, has
Gethsemane in mind. "Father, take this cup from me," Jesus prayed to "the
one who was able to save him from death, and he was heard." But the
answer to that prayer was not a simple change of mind on God's part,
"O.K., you don't have to die." Jesus had to enter fully into mortality, to die

and be buried. Then God's mighty power moved (or, more precisely, then God's mighty power continued to move) and death could not hold him. He was saved from death, but in God's way, not his own. He learned obedience, praying, "Not my will but yours be done," and so he becomes our teacher and model of prayer and obedient suffering by which we are brought to maturity, complete, even perfect by his great grace.

Because of what our high priest has done, mercy and grace are available to us "to help in time of need." Therefore, the writer to the Hebrews urges, "let us boldly approach the throne of grace" (4:16). Christ the high priest was also the victim offered in sacrifice. Some representations of the crucifixion show Jesus "reigning from the tree," crowned as king and dressed in the eucharistic vestments of a Christian priest. His body in these representations is not contorted in death but is alive, head high, eyes open, arms extended not in agony but in a wide invitation, "Come to me, all who are heavy laden," reaching out to embrace all who approach him. Thus we learn that it is the cross that is the throne of grace. We do not need to avert our eyes on Good Friday nor look beyond Golgotha to the "sapphire throne" of the Father far away in highest heaven to find the throne of grace. It is here on this hill outside Jerusalem, a hill that becomes the mountain of God and the source of mercy and forgiveness and gracious help. As the ancient hymn *Vexilla regis prodeunt* (referring to a supposed but nonexistent psalm verse) has it, "God is reigning from a tree."

The *Book of Common Prayer* since 1549 has appointed **Heb. 10:1-25** as the epistle for Good Friday. The passage is a full exposition of the surpassing perfection of the priesthood of Christ. The old sacrificial system is but a shadow compared to the reality that was to replace it. (1) The former system required repeated sacrifices "year after year" to deal with sin; Christ's sacrifice of himself was once for all, unrepeatable, "a full, perfect, and sufficient sacrifice, oblation, and satisfaction for the sins of the whole world," as Thomas Cranmer put it in the eucharistic prayer. (2) The old priests stood in daily service in a vain attempt to remove sin; Christ the priest having for all time offered his single sacrifice "sat down as a king at the right hand of God" (v. 12). (3) The old rites were external; the "new and living way" (v. 20) is written in the heart and requires a transformed life. This new covenant is made ours in baptism in which "our hearts are sprinkled clean . . . and our bodies washed with pure water" (v. 22). Lent finds its focus in preparation for or a renewal of baptism, and the premier time for baptism in all the year is at the Easter Vigil. This reading looks toward that personal appropriation of the death and resurrection of Christ by means of Holy Baptism.

GOSPEL: JOHN 18:1—19:42

The Gospel for Good Friday is the passion according to John, John 18:1—
19:42. It is fitting and noteworthy that it is this passion that is read on this
day every year rather than one of the Synoptic accounts. The choice of the
Johannine passion is more than a mechanical taking of the four Gospels in
order (in the medieval lectionaries Matthew was read on "Palm" Sunday,
Mark on Tuesday, Luke on Wednesday, John on Friday.) John's Gospel,
with its emphasis on the glory of the Son of God who moves majestically
through these events, is another indication that the appropriate mood for
Good Friday, God's Friday, is a restrained celebration. Jesus dies on the
cross, but as John tells the story, he dies with a shout of triumph on his lips,
"It is finished"; his work is completed, consummated. The redemption of
the universe has been accomplished, although at a fearsome cost.

The Johannine passion has as its focus the glory that radiates from the
self-assured Victim-Victor. After the last supper Jesus goes with his disciples to the garden. Judas brings a detachment of soldiers together with the
temple police to look for Jesus. Their frail lanterns and torches are a pitiful,
even ludicrous attempt to locate him who is the light of the world. Jesus,
"knowing all that was to happen to him" (nothing comes as a surprise,
especially in these last hours), goes boldly to them who on their own could
not find him. He says, "I am [he]." "He" is not present in the Greek, which
has simply, "I am," recalling the harsh debate reported in John 8 that reaches its climax in 8:58, "Before Abraham was, I am." Jesus' repeated use of
the divine name YHWH, "I AM WHO I AM" (Exod. 3:14) throughout this
Gospel asserts his claim to divinity and oneness with God. With the utter-
ance of that name, "I am," Jesus knocks the soldiers and police flat. They
fall to the ground as those who have seen God.

Before the high priest, Jesus gives instructions about whom he should
question. Because of his answer Jesus is struck on the face, of course, but
his cool and logical reply, "If I am wrong show me; if I am correct why
strike me?" ends the interview.

Pilate in his judicial way tries to cut to the heart of the matter with what
he thinks is the key question, "Are you the king of the Jews?" But Jesus'
response is a more searching interrogation of Pilate (and indirectly of all
who read or hear this story), "Do you ask this on your own, or did others
tell you about me?" We can almost sympathize with Pilate who is having
great difficulty getting a straight answer from this defendant. It is indeed
Pilate who is on trial. He is the prisoner of his own limitations, and it is
Jesus who is judge. Pilate persists in his efforts to set Jesus free, declaring
three times that there is "no case against him." At last, he delivers Jesus to
the mob with his repeated confession, "Here is your king."

Jesus goes to the Place of the Skull, carrying his own cross, like Isaac the intended victim carrying the wood on which he was to be sacrificed (Gen. 22:6). The glorious king goes confidently to Calvary "carrying the cross by himself," perhaps as a dramatization of what he has said earlier in the Gospel, "I lay down my life in order to take it up again . . . I lay it down of my own accord. I have power to lay it down, and I have power to take it up again" (John 10:17-18).

He dies with a shout of fulfillment, "It is finished!" and, having declared that the divine purpose has been accomplished, he "gave up [that is, handed over] his spirit," as if he could decide which was to be his final breath. The majestic priest and king has been in charge throughout, from arrest even to the moment of death.

A second fruitful approach to this passion account derives from the chronology peculiar to John. The Synoptics identify the last supper with the Passover meal. In John, Jesus died at the very time when the Passover lambs were being killed (John 18:28; 19:14). It may be, as some argue, that John is accurate in his presentation of historical facts here, but most students of the Bible would agree that John is less interested in historical accuracy than in the truth of theological ideas. It is not, the preacher must be careful to understand, a matter of fact versus fiction here requiring us to reject one account and embrace the other. All four Gospels are interested in truth. The Synoptics present truth one way; the Fourth Gospel presents it another way. Both can be (and Christianity would argue, are) correct and reliable, full of truth (John 1:14; 19:35). The story of the salvation of the world is so rich that no one approach can exhaust its meanings.

At the beginning of the Fourth Gospel, John the Baptist, seeing Jesus (significantly "coming toward him"), declares, "Here is the Lamb of God who takes away the sin of the world!" (1:29). This becomes a primary metaphor for this Gospel's presentation of the teaching and work of Jesus Christ, who is at once lamb and shepherd (10:11; Heb. 13:20; 1 Peter 2:25) as well as the gate for the sheep (10:7). He is "like a lamb that is led to the slaughter" (Isa. 53:7). Jesus died as the Passover lamb, a "lamb without blemish" (1 Peter 1:19), whose blood marks the doors of his people so that the angel of (eternal) death will pass over them. His death saves his people from death, his life substituted for theirs. And, like the Passover lamb, he himself becomes food for his people. The observance of this Passover becomes a perpetual ordinance (Exod. 12:14). The lamb whose death is sacrificial and redemptive is therefore also the lamb who conquers (Rev. 5:6, 12; 12:11; 13:8). As the Father is supreme in power, so the lamb, going forth to sacrifice, is supreme in love; and, ultimately, the power and the love are one.

Jesus moves majestically through this account of the passion, and yet he is the sacrificial lamb. John's emphasis on Jesus' regal power and glory throughout the Gospel does not, however, decrease human responsibility for the awful act. John, the apostle of love, is the harshest of the four evangelists in speaking of Judas, who he says is a "devil" (6:70; 13:2, 27).

It is John's continual blaming of "the Jews" that requires careful treatment by the preacher. "The Jews" is John's shorthand way of referring to the leaders of the Jewish people, primarily the chief priests and the scribes, and the responsible preacher must go out of the way to make that clear. Hostility between church and synagogue lie behind John's apparent contempt, the frustration of an increasingly separate church at the incredulity, which many saw as hard-hearted refusal, to acknowledge Jesus as Messiah, and the expulsion of some Christians from the synagogue. The preacher need not, indeed should not, deal directly with this issue in every Good Friday sermon, but the preacher must first understand what John means and how his phrase may be heard by modern congregations, and then be careful to avoid language that perpetuates misunderstanding. A useful way of being sensitive to the language one chooses is to imagine, as one prepares a sermon, that one's Jewish friends (or, if there are none, that a friendly delegation from a synagogue or temple) are in the congregation listening respectfully but critically to what one says.

There are certain distinctive and peculiar Johannine touches to which the preacher may choose to give attention. In Mark's passion, read on Sunday, there may be the author's self-portrayal and authentication in the unnamed and otherwise unidentified young man who fled naked from the scene of Jesus' arrest (Mark 14:51-52). So in the Fourth Gospel the nameless "disciple whom Jesus loved" (19:26), who may be the same person as "another disciple" (18:15) known to the high priest, may be the evangelist's portrait of himself. Another intriguing shadowy figure is the slave of the high priest, a relative of Malchus, whose ear Peter cut off (18:26, 10). And there is Barabbas, freed instead of Jesus, with the striking detail given by the evangelist as he dismisses him, "Now Barabbas was a bandit"; he stole the freedom that should rightfully have belonged to Jesus. Yet, in a wondrous conundrum, had Jesus been set free, there would have been no redemption.

Pilate is a fruitful subject for a character study. "Everyone who belongs to the truth listens to my voice," Jesus says to him (18:37). There are strong suggestions throughout this passion that Pilate had at least a dim sense of Jesus' importance in establishing a very different kind of kingdom than Pilate had ever known. In this verse Jesus may be appealing to an inner voice that has made its way into Pilate's consciousness. Pilate may have come close to understanding, but he abruptly closes off the dawning realization with the curt and cynical dismissal, "What is truth?" Sympathy gave way to expedience, possibility gave way to security, and Pilate has made the great refusal.

Or are we perhaps to hear this as one more question from Pilate who persistently kept trying to get a straight and understandable answer from Jesus? "Are you the king of the Jews?" "What have you done?" "So you are a king?" "What is truth?" Perhaps the question is meant earnestly. But it gets no response from Jesus. In his dramatic fashion, which we have seen so often in the Fourth Gospel, the evangelist lets the question hang there, unanswered, a perpetual challenge to all who hear the story.

John alone reports the tender scene at the cross when Jesus shows concern for his mother and for "the disciple whom he loved," commending them to each other's care. The passage shows Jesus' human compassion, even while in the agony of crucifixion. Some have seen in the maternal function of Mary a sign of the role of the church that was about to be born: "here is your mother" (19:27).

Nothing is simple in the Fourth Gospel, which abounds in symbolism. The spear that opens Jesus' side causing the double flood of blood and water shows not only that Jesus was really dead—a necessary assertion in the Christian creed—but in the context of Good Friday also points to baptism and the Holy Communion. Anciently, the baptismal preparation of Lent was drawing to a close and candidates were about to undergo, on the following evening at the Great Vigil of Easter, their initiation into the body of Christ by the washing of Holy Baptism and by their first reception of the Holy Communion. Moreover, in this Gospel water is a sign of the outpouring of the Holy Spirit and blood a symbol of the covenant sealed by the sacrificial death of the new paschal lamb (19:36; Exod. 12:46).

Finally, the universal character of the rule of this king is underscored. Crowned (with thorns) and robed in royal purple (19:2), this king stands before the representative of the Roman Empire, challenging its formidable might. Again and again Pilate refers to him as a king. The inscription that Pilate has written for the cross was in the three languages of the area—Hebrew, Latin, and Greek—so that everyone who passed by would know not just the charge but the proper title of this ruler whose power and authority come not from this world. Unlike all the kingdoms of the world, his is an imperishable and universal kingdom.

The liturgy of the Passion and Death of Our Lord Jesus Christ, the Good Friday service, does not come to a close. There is no conclusion, for the story is not yet finished. The narrative may pause for a while as we ponder the awesome events on Golgotha, but there is more to be told. This day yields to the dread silence of the Great Sabbath, Holy Saturday, a day of anticipation, of waiting for God to act and fulfill the ancient promises. Then Good Friday finds its conclusion and its interpretation in the awe-inspiring dramatic events and proclamation of the Great Vigil of Easter with which the Triduum ends and with which the celebration of Easter begins. In that powerful service the progression is from darkness to light, from slavery to freedom, from death to life. It is not just a new beginning but a breakthrough into a whole new dimension of existence. It is the entrance into what the New Testament calls eternal life. Such is the meaning of the Christian celebration of the passion and death of Christ.

The Great Vigil of Easter

Lectionary	Service of Readings		Second Lesson	Gospel
Revised Common	Gen. 1:1—2:4a	Bar. 3:9-15, 32—4:4	Rom. 6:3-11	Mark 16:1-8
	Gen. 7:1-5, 11-18;	Ezek. 36:24-28		
	8:6-18; 9:8-13	Ezek. 37:1-14		
	Gen. 22:1-18	Zeph. 3:14-20		
	Exod. 14:10-31,	Jonah 3:1-10		
	15:20-21	Deut. 31:19-30		
	Isa. 55:1-11	Dan. 3:1-29		
Episcopal (BCP)	Gen. 1:1—2:2	Isa. 4:2-6	Rom. 6:3-11	Matt. 28:1-10
	Gen. 7:1-5, 11-18;	Isa. 55:1-11		
	8:6-18; 9:8-13	Ezek. 36:24-28		
	Gen. 22:1-18	Ezek. 37:1-14		
	Exod. 14:10—15:1	Zeph. 3:12-20		
Roman Catholic	Gen. 1:1—2:2	Isa. 55:1-11	Rom. 6:3-11	Mark 16:1-7
	Gen. 22:1-18	Bar. 3:9-15, 32—4:4		
	Exod. 14:10—15:1	Ezek. 36:16-17a,		
	Isa. 54:5-14	18-28		
Lutheran (LBW)	Gen. 1:1—2:3	Isa. 55:1-11	I Cor. 15:19-28	Mark 16:1-8
	Gen. 7:1-5, 11-18;	Bar. 3:9-37		
	8:6-18; 9:8-13	Ezek. 37:1-14		
	Gen. 22:1-18	Jonah 3:1-10		
	Exod. 13:17—15:1	Deut. 31:19-30		
	Isa. 4:2-6	Dan. 3:1-29		

The Great Vigil of Easter is the culmination not only of the six weeks of
Lenten preparation; it is the climax of the entire Christian year. This mag-
nificent ritual, packed with deep and ancient symbols, gathers into one celebration the essence of Christianity. The whole history of salvation is told
in symbol and words and actions: striking the new fire, bringing light into
the darkness; praising the Easter candle which shows Passover and resurrection and the hope of all creation; reading from the biblical record, inter-
spersed with interpretative song and prayer; baptizing new Christians; eating and drinking the new life in the risen Christ. Christians have been
doing such things on this night at least since the fourth century, and millennia of universal religious impulses lie behind the Christian use.

The vigil begins in the darkness and desolation of Holy Saturday. Fire is
kindled, light leaps up, a great candle is lighted, and by its light lessons
from the Bible are read.

SERVICE OF READINGS

GENESIS 1:1—2:3 (—3:24). The first lesson in all four lectionaries is the
(first) story of creation, Gen. 1:1—2:3. The reading is a poetic statement of

what has just been dramatized with the new fire. The congregation has gathered in darkness, a light is kindled and spread through the church, driving back the shadows. So this grand hymn of creation explicates what the congregation has just experienced: they have, as it were, been present at the creation. They have experienced the primordial darkness with its emptiness, desolation, and horror. They have seen the effect of the majestic command, "Let there be light!" and as the light spreads, shattering the shadows, objects and people emerge from nothingness as at the beginning. At the divine Word, creatures leap into being.

The first chapter of Genesis is the grander and more majestic of the two stories that are woven together at the beginning of the Bible. The opening chapters of Genesis, 1–11, tell a primordial history that provides a universal setting for what is to become the early history of a particular people. Thus, these chapters, and in particular this first chapter of Genesis, are an appropriate beginning for the Bible (both the Hebrew Bible and the Christian extension of it) and for the celebration of the death and resurrection of Christ. We have already seen in many of the readings for Holy Week this universal aspect of the work of God in Christ. These various readings come to a focus, as the Easter Vigil begins, in reflection upon the beginning of the universe. A basic concept is laid out at the very beginning: the progress from chaos to cosmos, from nothing to something, from disorder to order, from emptiness to being. It is the great sweeping movement of the Bible, of the history of salvation, of the passion of Christ. It is a grand drama that turns out well and concludes with the reintegration of all creation. It is, in that sense, indeed a divine comedy.

The story begins before time began, in primeval chaos without form or order. Into the awesome emptiness, swept with the wind-breath-spirit from God, a Word is spoken and order begins. First darkness is separated from light; then the waters above are separated from the waters below by the dome of the sky; then the dry land is separated from the seas. It is not a wholly comforting picture. The darkness remains at night; great waters remain above the dome of the sky and below the earth and threaten to break loose and drown the world. The seas, remnants of the original chaos, remain menacingly at the edge of the earth and can flood the dry land and obliterate the separation of earth and sea, cancelling creation. This tenuous beginning will nearly come to ruin in the great flood, and it is also for us in our time a reminder of the fragility of our planet and life on it.

After the actions of separation, the created spaces are then filled with life. Vegetation covers the dry land; lights are hung in the sky—sun, moon, and stars; the waters swarm with living creatures, and the air is filled with birds; animals appear on the earth. Finally, as the crowning act of creation, human beings are made, "in the image of God." Male and female are given supremacy, dominion, and control over the rest of creation. Their role is to act as viceroys of God on earth, and yet, as if to remind them of their subordinate place, human beings are not made on a day of their own. They share their day of creation with the animals.

Until God spoke it was a cold and desolate and forbidding scene. Then God's wind-breath-spirit-word-life enlivened and enlightened the chaos with divine creative and sustaining power. The work of creation is reviewed and recalled not only each week but each day. The dawn of history is recalled at the dawn of each day as the first light slowly reveals the outline of the earth, the sun emerges, and at last—in agricultural communities at least—people begin their work.

The recurring refrain through this chapter is the statement of God's approval. "And God saw that it was good" (only the second day lacks such a blessing). But after human beings have been made and creation is complete, the Creator looks at everything and "indeed, it was very good." The artist is pleased with the work. There is a moral emphasis here too: the creation at its completion is entirely good; there is, as yet, no imperfection, no sin. That will come later, in Genesis 3 (part of the longer reading appointed by the *Lutheran Book of Worship*), and it will come from the outside. Sin emphatically was not part of the original creation as that work came from God's hand. In its newly minted glory with the glow of a fresh spring day, creation was good; it was very good.

As the story of creation began before time began, so the concluding verses (2:1-3) serve as a timeless epilogue to the mighty work. On the seventh day God rested. In the context of the Easter Vigil this divine rest is more than the pattern and model for the sabbath rest, for this day is the Great Sabbath, the day of rest for Christ after the supreme work of remaking the cosmos. His labor finished, he lies in the darkness and silence of the tomb until again a divine command is spoken and light shines in the darkness once more, and life arises from death. As John makes clear in the prologue to his Gospel, light and life are interchangeable: "In him was life, and the life was the light of all people" (John 1:4). This light, this life is not merely renewal, as the dawn of one day succeeds the last, but this light which is life is a breaking out of the confinement of space and time into a new and nearly unimaginable dimension that we know as resurrection.

The *Lutheran Book of Worship* provides as an option Gen. 1:1—3:24, extending the first account of creation to include the second account (2:4-25), which stresses the lowliness of humanity, made of the dust of the ground, susceptible to temptation, and includes also the account of the fall into sin (chap. 3) by succumbing to temptation. It was the fall of humanity that required a divine redeemer, "Our Lord Jesus Christ, who paid for us the debt of Adam to the eternal Father and who by his precious blood redeemed us from the bondage to the ancient sin," as the grand Easter proclamation, the *Exsultet*, declares.

A focus of Genesis 3 is the tree of disobedience, the tree of the knowledge of good and evil, which brought death into paradise; at Good Friday-Easter the focus is on the tree of obedience, the cross, which brought life to a dying world and which opened paradise. The collect that follows this reading from Genesis in the *Book of Common Prayer* and in the *Lutheran Book of Worship* makes the connection between the fall of humanity and the work of Christ, praying to God, "who wonderfully created, and yet more wonderfully restored, the dignity of human nature."

GENESIS 7:1-5, 11-18; 8:6-18; 9:8-13. The *Lutheran Book of Worship, Book of Common Prayer,* and the Revised Common Lectionary provide the story of the great flood (Gen. 7:1-5, 11-18, 8:6-18, 9:8-13) as an optional reading for the Vigil. The newly created world was a fragile work. The opening verses of Genesis, describing creation, describe the precarious situation of the world with the menace of darkness and flood not far removed from it, threatening it from the edges. It is still so. We have seen photographs of the blue earth, an island of life floating in the blackness of space. Ancient pictures continue to speak with renewed power.

According to Genesis 1 creation was "good", but now "the earth was corrupt in God's sight" (6:11), and God now moves to unmake creation. Paradise was lost because of sin, and the state of the world declined. The young world was nearly destroyed as the waters above flooded down and the waters beneath the earth welled up and the order of the cosmos reverted to the chaos of the flood. Only those safe in the ark survived, the progenitors of a new world and a new humanity (1 Peter 3:20-21). Noah's flood in the context of the Easter Vigil is a figure of baptism. Water can destroy, but water can also save. Sin is drowned and new life is brought forth from the water as at the beginning (1:20). It is a renewal of creation, a reordering of the chaos, a new beginning of the earth. As at the beginning (1:2), God "made a wind blow over the earth" (8:1) and order returns. The original command is renewed, "Be fruitful and multiply" (8:17). A covenant is made with all humanity, indeed, with all creation, animals as well as humans. God's rule is universal, and under that rule a predictable and generally dependable order is established. The sign of this covenant is the (rain)bow in the sky. It arches there, a weapon hung up after its use, as a sign of God's judgment and mercy.

GENESIS 22:1-18. All four lectionaries appoint the story of Abraham's aborted sacrifice of Isaac, Gen. 22:1-18. It is the most profound experience in the whole history of the patriarchs. Abraham obeys God's command to take the only child he and Sarah had, a beloved son, the only possible link with the posterity that had been promised, and to offer him as a sacrifice. It was heroic of Abraham to start out for the unspecified "place I will show you" (Gen. 12:1); it is a far more daunting challenge to maintain hope when all seemed about to be destroyed.

The narrative is a masterpiece of storytelling. When God gives the appalling command, Abraham silently obeys. For three days the silence is oppressive. Then Abraham breaks it: "The boy and I will . . . worship, and then we will come back to you" (22:5). It is a lie, for Abraham cannot bring himself to say then that only one of them will return; but it is in fact the truth: father and son will both return safely. Abraham loads up his son with the wood as if he were a beast of burden, distancing himself as best he can from the deed he has been commanded to do, as if Isaac were not a child but an animal for sacrifice. Abraham himself, in a chilling detail without need of comment, "carried the fire and the knife." "Where is the lamb?" the apprehensive child asks. "God will provide," the father answers evasively, but twice he calls Isaac "my son." His attempt to see his son as an animal has failed, and his paternal love prevails. Abraham passes the test. His obedient faith has been proved, and a ram replaces the son.

Read at the Easter Vigil this lesson points toward a greater sacrifice. Moriah, an unidentified location where Abraham was commanded to take his son, was later identified with the temple mount in Jerusalem (2 Chron. 3:1). The gloss on the name, "On the mountain of the LORD it will be provided" (Gen. 22:14), thus looks forward to the temple and in the context of the Easter Vigil looks further to Mount Calvary where God provides a Son to replace all the sacrifices of old. Moreover, the theme of the deliverance of the firstborn is common to the sacrifice of Isaac, Passover, and the crucifixion. God rescued from death Isaac, Israel, and Christ.

EXODUS (13:17—)14:10—15:1. All four lectionaries appoint the story of the passage through the Red Sea, Exod. 14:10—15:1 (the *Lutheran Book of Worship* begins the reading at 13:17). Indeed, this reading is required in the *Roman Sacramentary*, the *Book of Common Prayer*, and the *Lutheran Book of Worship*, for it is the central story of the Hebrew Bible for this night of passage, the decisive act of deliverance. It is not a story of escape from prison as if the Hebrews by good fortune or by their cleverness were able to slip out of Egypt when their captors were not paying attention. Their deliverance was not their own doing. Their freedom was a gift, entirely undeserved, a victory for the unequaled might of their God. This intervention on their behalf is the formative event of ancient Israel, and it made of them a nation.

The intervention was decisive for it not only delivered them from their former life of slavery, but with a wall of water prevented their return to what was not their home and led them through the years of preparation to their own land.

The narrative moves quickly. The desperate situation of the Hebrews is emphasized at the beginning of chap. 14. They were trapped between Egyptian frontier forts and the sea. The lesson begins with the Israelites with their backs to the water and "the Egyptians advancing on them" (v. 10). The fearful Israelites with their short memory cry out to Moses, "We told you so. We were better off in Egypt." Moses' threefold reply is "Do not be afraid, stand firm, and see the deliverance that the LORD will accomplish for you today" (v. 13).

(a) There was every reason to be afraid. Their destruction seemed imminent. Yet, in the face of apparently certain death, Moses' command was, "Do not be afraid." It is a command that runs through the entire Bible to encourage people faced with disturbing situations they cannot understand with human reason. When God appeared to Abram, the patriarch was told, "Do not be afraid" (Gen. 15:1; also 26:24). Samuel says the same to the repentant people of Israel in his farewell address (1 Sam. 12:20). Jonathan encouraged David with these words in the Wilderness of Ziph (1 Sam. 23:17). Elisha strengthened his servant with these words when the Aramean army had them surrounded (2 Kings 6:16). "Do not be afraid" is the beginning of the angel's address to Zechariah (Luke 1:13) and to Mary (Luke 1:30) and to the shepherds (Luke 2:10). It is the word of the risen Lord to the women at the tomb (Matt. 28:10) and to Paul under persecution (Acts 18:9) and to John the Divine (Rev. 1:17). (See also Isa. 35:4; 41:10; Jer. 1:8; Ezek. 2:6; Matt. 14:27; Mark 5:36.)

(b) The people are to show their courage by standing firm, Moses' second command. It is a command for people to be expectant. The prophet Jahaziel said to Judah and Jerusalem, "This battle is not for you to fight; take your position, stand still, and see the victory of the LORD on your behalf" (2 Chron. 20:17). Samuel said to Saul as he was about to anoint him king of Israel, "Tell the boy to go on before us, and when he has passed on, stop here yourself for a while, that I may make known to you the word of God" (1 Sam. 9:27). Samuel in his farewell address to Israel says, "Now therefore take your stand and see this great thing that the LORD will do before your eyes" (1 Sam. 12:16). Advent is characterized by such expectancy, but Holy Saturday is the supreme day of standing expectantly, keeping vigil through the night for the first signs of the light of the resurrection.

(*c*) The result of the people's expectant waiting is that they see their deliverance. Their fear is banished, their longing is satisfied, their hope is fulfilled. They become eyewitnesses to God's work. All they can do is stand and watch as their deliverance is accomplished. In the Orthodox churches when the priest gives Holy Communion to communicants, he says, "The servant of God partakes of the precious and holy body and blood of our Lord and God and Savior, Jesus Christ, unto the remission of sin and unto life everlasting." The priest who presides at the Divine Liturgy is but a witness to the communication as he is at a baptism, saying not "I baptize you" but "The servant of God is baptized. . . ." Priest and congregation stand back in reverence and watch the miraculous encounter.

God told Moses, "Now you shall see what I will do to Pharaoh" (Exod. 6:1). When the covenant is renewed later in Exodus, God declares to the Hebrews, "I will perform marvels . . . and all the people among whom you live shall see the work of the LORD" (Exod. 34:10). This seeing is more than merely watching. It is being an eyewitness to great and awesome deeds.

Earlier, the contest had been between Moses, God's magician with his rod, and Pharaoh's magicians. The Egyptian sorcerers matched Moses deed for deed, turning their staves into snakes (Exod. 7:10-11), turning the water of the Nile into blood (7:20-22), bringing frogs over the land (8:6-7). But then the powers of the Egyptians failed. Moses alone could bring gnats and flies, disease, boils, thunder and hail, locusts, thick darkness. Now at the sea it becomes a contest between Pharaoh himself and the Lord—two powerful gods fighting each other for supremacy. The Egyptians, pursuing the Hebrews, "went into the sea after them." Caught in the mud, they could not escape, and the sea closed over them. Israel was saved but at the cost of enemy lives: "Israel saw the Egyptians dead on the seashore" (v. 30). Israel saw the great work, "so the people feared the LORD" (v. 31). Thus victory is not just a cause for rejoicing; it is a costly victory. Freedom must be bought at the price of human lives. Some are saved; others die. It is difficult for us to read this gloatingly. No wonder the people "feared the LORD." Here on the far shore of this sea is an awesome display of power beyond human control and even beyond human comprehension.

All this happened "at the morning watch" (14:24), and the story is read at the Great Watch, the vigil of Easter. As the *Exsultet* sings repeatedly, "This is the night." The victory at the sea is won during the night. Mysterious acts shrouded in darkness recall the night of the Passover in which all the firstborn die and the night in which Christ's resurrection took place. When morning breaks over the sea, the sun rises on a scene of destruction and deliverance.

The narrative of the passage through the sea is not to be understood as an isolated lection, a self-contained story. It is the formative event of

ancient Israel as the passion-resurrection is the formative event of the
church and as baptism is the formative event of individual Christians. It is
all one story. All the stories coalesce this night and all are commemorated
together. Bible and Israel and church and individual combine. Those who
are to be baptized at the vigil as well as those who have previously been
baptized have joined themselves to a long history.

The song of Miriam and Moses (Exodus 15) follows this lesson as an
extension of it, a comment on it, and a celebration of God's saving power.

Isaiah 4:2-6. The *Book of Common Prayer* and the *Lutheran Book of Worship* provide Isa. 4:2-6, a vision of God's presence in a renewed Israel and
of the restoration of Jerusalem after a time of cleansing and purification.
The connections between this lesson and what happens in baptism are the
point of this reading on this night: the fire that is a central symbol of the
liturgy of this night (and the clouds of incense) and the washing away of
filth and cleansing by a spirit of judgment and burning. In Holy Baptism
candidates are washed in the saving flood and are given the Holy Spirit.
The signs of God's presence, signs that led and protected the Hebrews and
that filled the tabernacle, the pillar of cloud and the pillar of fire, are
restored in the purified city and cover Mount Zion as a canopy, providing
shade from heat and shelter from storm. God's very presence will fill, surround, and protect the holy city, the true home of "everyone who has been
recorded for life in Jerusalem" (v. 3), the destiny of the baptized. And all of
these experiences—the miracles of the exodus, the vision of the restoration
of the holy city, the death and resurrection of Christ, the Easter Vigil, the
baptisms this night—become part of the history of each of the baptized and
each of the baptized is joined to this long and thrilling story.

Isaiah 54:5-14. The Roman Catholic lectionary appoints Isa. 54:5-14, a
portion of a poem of assurance to Israel. The poem puts the desolation of
the cross into the larger perspective of God's view. In the poem, God consoles Israel as a husband consoles a wife, who has been abandoned for a
brief moment, from whom "in overflowing wrath for a moment I hid my
face" (v. 8). The years of Israel's rejection are but a moment in God's
expansive view of time. There was estrangement but no divorce.

Christ's desolate and piercing cry from the cross, "My God, why have
you forsaken me?" (Ps. 22:1; Matt. 27:46; Mark 15:34) finds an answer in
this text. It suggests that God did for a brief moment turn away and abandon Christ, but God's love is nonetheless everlasting. From now on,
because of this terrifying moment of abandonment, the people of God will
never be without the steadfast love of God, and, the Lord promises, "my

covenant of peace shall not be removed" (v. 10). Oppression and terror will be kept far away.

Isaiah 55:1-11. All the lectionaries appoint Isa. 55:1-11, an invitation to accept as a gift that which is freely offered by God. In the context of the Easter Vigil, this reading is to be heard as God's invitation, extended through the church, to "come to the waters," to the saving, renewing, life-giving waters of baptism. The washing in those baptismal waters is the gateway to the Lord's table. Here at this royal banquet, in the reading and in the congregation, is rich food—wine and milk without cost and bread that can satisfy the needs of those who are about to partake of the Holy Communion for the first time. It is an offer of life, an extension of the covenant established with David to include David's people, Israel, and further extended in King David's greater Son. Those who are being initiated into the power and majesty of God by means of the Christian mysteries this night are being so glorified that nations will gather because of the great deeds of this holy night.

The lesson is also for those who have long been baptized members of the Christian community. "Return to the Lord" (v. 7), who is rich in mercy and who will abundantly pardon those who return in this time of grace. Repentance requires a complete change not only in conduct but in thoughts as well.

These great acts of grace, gathering new members and purifying the old are the wonderful work of the Word of God, that having been spoken is already at work and that will not return to God empty. It is the same Word that called the worlds into being, beginning, as the first reading for the Vigil declares, "Let there be light." It is the Word that continues to sustain the universe. That divine Word is always effective. It cannot fail to do what it was spoken to accomplish, for it has been spoken by God and is therefore filled with divine intention and power. The celebration of this night is a celebration of the continuing power, certain and sure, of the Word first spoken at the beginning of creation, the Word that continues throughout Scripture, and that is undiminished in power even in our own day. Now, as salvation is about to be realized, made real and perceived, in the resurrection and in the baptism of new Christians, we are taught that there are no barriers to this life except those erected by our own rejection of the offer.

Baruch 3:9-15, 32—4:4. The *Lutheran Book of Worship*, the *Roman Sacramentary*, and the Revised Common Lectionary appoint Bar. 3:9-15, 32—4:4, a poem in praise of wisdom as embodied in the law, the life-giving commandments of God.

This lesson is directed toward those who, like Israel in exile, are as yet captive to a dying world. Captivity and death are the inevitable result of forsaking the fountain of wisdom. The previous reading from Isaiah 55 declared, "Come to the waters." This lesson from Baruch is for those who have not accepted the invitation.

Obedience to the law is the means by which Israel may partake of the fullness of life with abundant joy and gladness. In a Christian context, Christ, who is the fulfillment of the law, is Holy Wisdom and the source of strength, understanding, length of days, light, and peace. Turn, take, walk toward that shining light.

EZEKIEL 36:[16-23] 24-28. The *Roman Sacramentary*, the *Book of Common Prayer*, and the Revised Common Lectionary appoint Ezek. 36:[16-23]24-28. The message given by God to Ezekiel is a promise of cleansing, renewal, and restoration. The lost and the scattered will be gathered and brought back into their own land. Because sinners cannot cleanse themselves (the background is Num. 19:9-22) God promises to wash them and give them a new heart and spirit, which are in fact God's heart and God's spirit. The heart, in ancient Hebrew understanding is the seat of knowing and willing; the promised "heart of flesh" implies a sensitive and receptive heart.

The promise, according to a Christian understanding, is fulfilled in Holy Baptism by which exiled sinners are brought home, cleansed and given the Holy Spirit. Again, the words are heard as addressed to the candidates for baptism, who are about to be given a new heart and a new spirit, and to those who are already within the Christian church and who this night are being called to renew their baptismal commitment.

EZEKIEL 37:1-14. The *Lutheran Book of Worship*, the *Book of Common Prayer*, and the Revised Common Lectionary appoint the story of Ezekiel's vision of the valley of the dry bones, Ezek. 37:1-14. After a series of somber and intense readings, this amusing vision comes as welcome relief. The valley is an old battlefield where a great army was slaughtered long ago (the bones were "very dry"). Not a drop of moisture remains; the bones are scattered; all hope of life is gone. Yet, at the word of the prophet, the scattered bones begin to move and with a great clattering the bones joined together to form skeletons. (We cannot help at least smiling as we imagine the picture.) Then from the inside out—sinews, then flesh, then skin—bodies were reconstituted. Finally, filled with breath-wind-spirit, the bodies stand up, "a vast multitude."

In Ezekiel's prophecy, Israel in exile, all hope gone, and, contrary to all logic and sense, will be restored and returned to their own land. The promise of life is to "the whole house of Israel" wherever they live in exile as well as those who remain in the land. So at the Easter Vigil, Christians who have lost loved ones, whose strength is declining, even those who are spiritually dead have the hope not just of life but "the resurrection of the body," as the Apostles' Creed confesses.

ZEPHANIAH 3:12-20. The readings are becoming more confident and more joyful as the Vigil progresses. The *Book of Common Prayer* and the Revised Common Lectionary appoint Zeph. 3:12-20, an account of the gathering of God's people. Zion's song of rejoicing is a celebration of the enthronement and rule of God. Israel, no longer a mere remnant, is urged to sing and shout with joy for the true King of Israel, the Lord God, "a warrior who gives victory," is in their midst. Shame has been turned into praise, exile into homecoming, contempt into renown, poverty into riches, desolation into restoration. The Shepherd has gathered the scattered flock. For many of the prophets (e.g., Zeph. 1:9-10) "that day" is the day of retribution and doom. But now it is a time of gladness announced by the encouraging command, "Do not fear." Christ, as the *Te Deum* sings, "overcame the sting of death and opened the kingdom of heaven to all believers."

JONAH 3:1-10. The *Lutheran Book of Worship* and the Revised Common Lectionary, following the medieval vigil, appoint Jonah 3:1-10, the reluctant prophet's conversion of Nineveh, turning them—all of them from the king even to the animals—to repentance. Jonah has been regarded as a "type" of Christ, delivered from three days in the belly of the fish/earth, now with new life and power extending that resurrection to the Gentiles.

DEUTERONOMY 31:19-30. The *Lutheran Book of Worship* and the Revised Common Lectionary, following the medieval vigil, appoint Deut. 31:19-30, a passage introducing the Song of Moses. The reading looks ahead to the time when the Israelites are in their own land, enjoying its produce. Faced with such unaccustomed luxury, the people will turn away from their God, breaking the covenant. Then the Song of Moses will "confront them as a witness" (v. 21), condemning their faithlessness in the face of God's faithfulness.

In the Easter Vigil this passage is to be heard addressing those who have long been baptized, calling them to maintain the life to which they were committed at their baptism. The great stories from the past reviewed this night are read in part to renew their dedication and to restore their pride in being part of a noble and ancient tradition. "Remember the days of old, consider the years long past." Incidents of past rebellion and forgetfulness stand as warnings to those who by Holy Baptism become part of the continuing story of salvation, a story that is not yet finished.

DANIEL 3:1-29. The *Lutheran Book of Worship* and the Revised Common Lectionary appoint Dan. 3:1-29 as the final reading before the Eucharist begins, the rollicking story of the three youths in the furnace. The point is a serious and sober one: martyrdom is to be preferred to apostasy. But the delightful way in which the story is told is not to be shortchanged. In its leisurely way, the story with its exaggerations and repetitions suggests the grandeur of the kingdom of Nebuchadnezzar and recalls stories children enjoy when a passage they know begins again and they can join in.

The grand list of officials given in v. 2—"the satraps, the prefects, and the governors, the counselors, the treasurers, the justices, the magistrates, and all the officials of the provinces"—is repeated word for word in the next verse as they all obediently assemble. According to the royal proclamation, all "peoples, nations, and languages" (v. 4) are to worship the ninety-foot-high gilded statue when they hear "the sound of the horn, pipe, lyre, trigon, harp, drum, and entire musical ensemble" (v. 5). Two verses later the sound of "the horn, pipe, lyre, trigon, harp, drum, and entire musical ensemble" announces the worship of the golden statue. Three verses later the list of instruments is repeated again in the report that "certain Jews" (we hear the hiss of anti-Semitism) pay no heed to the royal decree. Yet again (v. 15) King Nebuchadnezzar reminds the three young men of the list of instruments that announce a time of worship. The three, refusing sacrilegious worship, were thrown into "the furnace of blazing fire"; the formula is repeated again and again (vv. 6, 11, 15). The furnace of blazing fire, heated seven times more than usual, was so hot that it killed the men who threw Shadrach, Meshach, and Abednego into it. The curious king looks in and sees not three but four men walking in the furnace, "and the fourth has the appearance of a god" (it was apparently an angel). The three youths came out safely. Nebuchadnezzar's comment on the event, "There is no other god who is able to deliver in this way" (v. 29), is on this night to be heard as true of the God who delivered Christ from the sure destruction of the grave. The glorious *Benedicite omnia opera*, the song of the three youths with its repetitions that are now majestic rather than amusing, is sung in response to this reading.

The service of readings, now concluded, has had as its purpose a review of the history of salvation as the context for baptism. The next action of the

Great Vigil of Easter is the baptism of candidates and the renewal of baptismal vows of those who have previously been baptized. Then the first Eucharist of Easter begins.

SECOND READING: ROMANS 6:3-11

The epistle appointed in the *Roman Sacramentary*, the *Book of Common Prayer*, and the Revised Common Lectionary is Rom. 6:3-11, an almost inevitable choice given the context of this night, Paul's explication of the relationship between baptism and the death and resurrection of Christ. (It was the epistle for the Easter Vigil in the Mozarabic rite.) The reader addresses the whole congregation, including those who have just been baptized, saying in the words of Paul, "all of us who have been baptized into Christ Jesus . . . have been buried with him by baptism" (v. 3). The plural pronouns in Paul's letter have a special force and inclusiveness when read this night. The newly baptized hear them for the first time as Christians, members of the body of Christ. They who have been undergoing preparation have been made Christians and are now included as part of the church. Older Christians speak to younger, as Paul of centuries ago speaks still to Christians at the turn of the millennia. We are all part of one body. The basic Christian confession (1 Cor. 15:3-4)—the death, burial, and resurrection of Christ—is experienced in the new life of the baptized, who by their baptism participate in those central events.

Baptism is the Easter sacrament for in it and by it we participate in Christ's death and resurrection. Paul here probably has in mind baptism by immersion. Our old self dies, drowned in the cleansing waters, and we rise from the water to live with Christ. The union with Christ is more than a mystical identification; it is having a share in his death and resurrection. By baptism the sinful self is destroyed. As death clears all charges against a defendant, so the death in baptism makes a clear break from sin. It is a new person who rises from the water.

The reading concludes by speaking directly to the congregation, particularly to those who have just been baptized, shifting with strong effect from "we" to "you": "So you also must consider yourselves dead to sin and alive to God in Christ Jesus" (v. 11). Baptism has replaced one obedience with another, one life with another. The entire direction of the new Christians' lives has been transformed. They no longer live for themselves but for God; they live not only for God but more powerfully they live the life of Christ, the risen Lord who lives in them and through them. The radical demarcation marked by baptism could not be clearer. The ethical obligations of the new life are apparent: "How can we who died to sin go on living in it?" (v. 2). You enter the water and die with Christ, die to sin. You emerge from the water, rising with Christ to a new life of active obedience to God. Therefore, become what you are—people dead to sin and risen to new life.

Renewal of life is a present reality, although for Paul, resurrection is still a future event. The new life begins now, but it is brought to perfection in the life to come. "We believe that we will also live with him" (v. 8), beyond this mortal life, beyond the inevitable grave, beyond the limitations of space and time in a new world that surpasses our wildest imagination.

The *Lutheran Book of Worship* does not appoint an epistle or Gospel for the Vigil. The assumption is that those who celebrate the Easter Vigil will use the second lesson and Gospel appointed for Easter Day. For comment on the second lesson, 1 Cor. 15:19-28, see Easter Day, Year B.

GOSPEL: MARK 16:1-8

The appointed Gospel in the *Roman Sacramentary*, the *Lutheran Book of Worship*, and the Revised Common Lectionary is Mark 16:1-8. It is a mysterious and disturbing reading, and the preacher needs to be careful not to make it say more than it does. There is no appearance of Jesus; the appearances happen later. Although an anticipatory anointing had been done by the woman in Simon's house (Mark 14:3-9), in the Synoptic accounts of the burial of Jesus no mention is made of an anointing of Jesus' body (see John 19:40). As the sun rises Easter morning, three women (Mary Magdalene, Mary the mother of James, and Salome) come to the tomb to anoint the body of Jesus. They find the tomb open and a young man, an angel, sitting where Jesus had lain. He announces to them the nearly incomprehensible news that Jesus who was crucified had been raised. He was laid here—the angel points to the niche in the rock—but he is gone. They are looking in the wrong place. The women are to tell the disciples, and especially their leader Peter (Mark is "the interpreter of Peter" Papias reported), that they will see Jesus in Galilee, just as he said: "After I am raised up, I will go before you to Galilee" (Mark 14:28). His promise is dependable, despite crucifixion. The special charge to tell Peter, who just three days earlier had denied knowing Jesus, who was, we imagine, lost in grief and remorse over the part he had played in this tragedy that had ruined his life and the lives of those around him, must have cheered the apostle's heart and lifted him out of despair.

It is the concluding verse of this Gospel reading, which may have been the concluding verse of the Gospel in its original form, that is so disturbing. The women fled from the tomb in terror and amazement, saying nothing to anyone despite the angel's command, "for they were afraid." The women unexpectedly found themselves facing the result of something they could not comprehend. It filled them with a shuddering awe, for they were in the presence of the incomprehensible divine. When Jesus died with that piercing cry, "My God, why have you forsaken me?" we shudder at the terrifying scream. The centurion who saw how he died was moved to make his confession, "Truly this man was God's Son!" The human mind is inadequate to understand this awesome happening. Words fail in the presence of such divine action. Those who stood in the empty tomb Easter morning were overwhelmed. It was unlike anything they had experienced before, and so they were afraid. Christians at this Vigil (and if this is the Gospel read on Easter morning) need to stand with the women in a tomb where the body had been laid but now was no more and to contemplate in silence the fact of the empty tomb. The preacher should not introduce any appearances of the risen Jesus; there is time enough for that during the next weeks of Easter. On this night, to enliven and reinvigorate a story we know so well that we may not listen carefully to it any more, the preacher needs to confront the congregation with the evidence they have no way of processing. This is a night to stand trembling in holy fear.

It is not merely terrifying. There is hope also. The modern congregation cannot forget the facts it knows, cannot put out of mind the knowledge of the resurrection, cannot deny the appearances the risen Jesus makes to the disciples. We know that reliable people after Easter morning saw and even touched Jesus, who was undeniably alive. We depend on the testimony of those who saw and heard and touched him. But we do not see him, and the angel's message is for us still: "He is going ahead of you to Galilee; there you will see him" (v. 7).

"Galilee" in this saying has perplexed commentators through the centuries. Some have simply gotten rid of the troublesome verse by suggesting that it is a later addition. Such an approach has a suspect ease about it. Elsewhere in the Bible Jerusalem is the holy city, the sign and seat of God's presence on earth, the anticipation and promise of the peace of heaven. "I saw the holy city, the new Jerusalem, coming down out of heaven from God," John the Divine reports (Rev. 21:2). "The Jerusalem above . . . is our mother," Paul wrote to the Galatians (Gal. 4:26). But Jerusalem, especially in Mark's Gospel, is a place of opposition, unbelief, and death.

It is difficult to listen to this Gospel and not to hear the promise of meeting in Galilee as wonderfully encouraging. It is where Jesus had his early success in his ministry. We perhaps do not misunderstand if we hear "heaven" in the name "Galilee." When Jesus broke out of the tomb he did not simply resume work in Jerusalem that had been interrupted by his crucifixion. The resurrection broke through the barriers of space and time into a new dimension, and so Jesus broke out of the common expectations of Jerusalem and its centrality and its pride and self-satisfaction. He shattered the hold of death and instead of restoring the ancient kingdom in Jerusalem he went north to Galilee, a symbol for the Gentiles, "Galilee of the nations . . . of the Gentiles" (Isa. 9:1-2; Matt. 4:15). This is a new kind of king who rules over a new and universal kingdom, bright with youth and hope and joy. John Greenleaf Whittier in the hymn "Immortal Love, Forever Full," catches something of this suggestion:

> *Faith still has its Olivet,*
> *And love its Galilee.*

He has gone before us, and when we arrive, he will be there waiting for us. There we too will see him.

GOSPEL: MATTHEW 28:1-10

The *Book of Common Prayer* appoints Matt. 28:1-10 as the Gospel for the Great Vigil of Easter in all three years of the lectionary cycle. (It is appointed for Year A in the Roman Catholic and the Revised Common lectionaries.) It is an extension of the Gospel appointed for the Vigil since the earliest Roman lectionaries (28:1-7). The account is similar to Mark's with its picture of the empty tomb but with Matthew's special emphases. There was an earthquake, an angel rolled back the stone, the guards were stunned, the women left the tomb with fear and joy. The Prayer Book extends the reading through v. 10 to include an appearance of the risen Jesus. It is he, not an angel as in Mark, who meets the two women and gives them the message for the apostles to go to Galilee where they will see Jesus.

The promise of meeting the risen Savior (made sure by the testimony of eyewitnesses who in fact saw him and conversed with him) completes the transition from the darkness of Holy Week to the dawning light of Easter that extends throughout Bright Week (Easter Week) and the great Fifty Days of gladness and joy.